Classic
HOUSEHOLD HINTS

Classic HOUSEHOLD HINTS

OVER *500* OLD AND NEW

TIPS FOR A HAPPIER HOME

SUSAN WAGGONER

STEWART, TABORI & CHANG
NEW YORK

Published in 2007 by Stewart, Tabori & Chang
An imprint of Harry N. Abrams, Inc.

Library of Congress Cataloging-in-Publication Data

Waggoner, Susan.
  Classic household hints : over 500 old and new tips for a happier home.
    p. cm.
  Includes index.
  ISBN-13: 978-1-58479-572-8
  ISBN-10: 1-58479-572-7
  1. Home economics. I. Title.

TX158.W34 2006
640--dc22

2006033813

Editor: Dervla Kelly
Designer: Kay Schuckhart/Blond on Pond
Production Manager: Alexis Mentor

The text of this book was composed in Adobe Caslon

Printed in China
10 9 8 7 6 5 4 3 2 1

HNA
harry n. abrams, inc.
a subsidiary of La Martinière Groupe

115 West 18th Street
New York, NY 10011
www.hnabooks.com

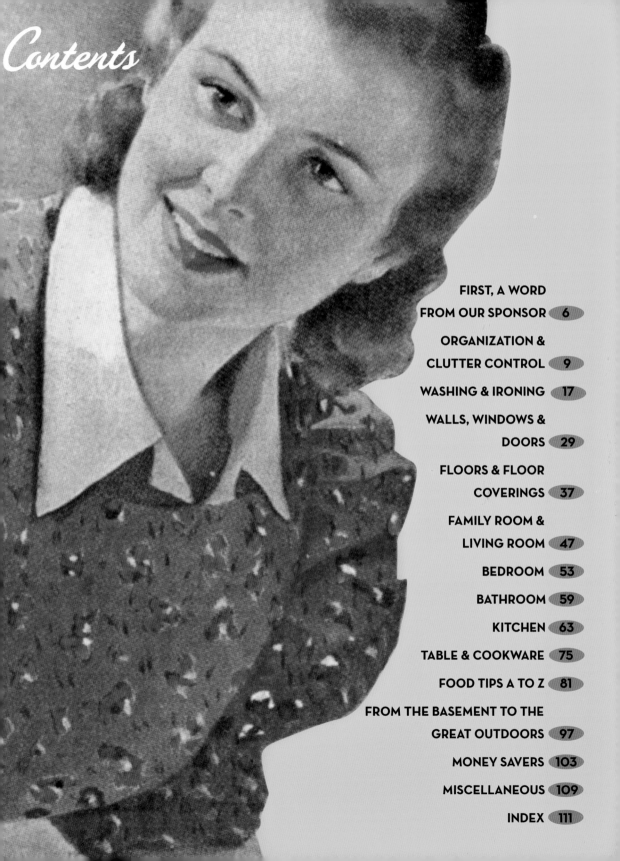

Contents

First, a word from our sponsor . . .

No one who has spent any time at all reading old housekeeping manuals can doubt that we live in an age of splendors. Today, when most of us think "roughing it" means doing dishes by hand rather than in the dishwasher, it's worth remembering that our grandmothers and great-grandmothers not only had to pump the water themselves; they then had to carry it into the kitchen, heat it, and later carry the dirty water back outside to dump it. One estimate, made at the end of the nineteenth century, found that the average homemaker walked 148 miles a year carrying 36 tons of water. She also spent four hours a day tending the stove. Not cooking on it—that was a whole other project—but just feeding it the 50 pounds of wood and coal it required daily, emptying its ash box, adjusting its dampers, and rubbing it with blacking to forestall rust.

Is it any wonder these women were constantly in search of shortcuts? Of products that would clean better, faster, and with less roughening of hands?

They were remarkably resourceful. In the absence of modern detergents, paper towels, Tupperware, spray cleaners, stain-resistant fabrics, non-porous counters, refrigeration, and electricity, they managed to raise our grandparents and great-grandparents without starving or poisoning anyone. When innovations came along, they made the most of them. The first

major electrical appliance, the wringer-
washer of the 1930s, was quickly retrofit-
ted to double as butter churn, ice-cream
maker, and meat grinder.

In the course of researching this book
and testing hundreds of tips, I learned to
be grateful—very grateful—for ordinary
miracles such as plastic containers, which
unlike their wood and glass predecessors,
did not have crevices where bacteria could
multiply in deadly force, and would not
shatter when they slipped
from young fingers that
had reached for them
too eagerly. The bottom
line is: We may mourn
the passing of home
milk delivery, but no one
misses finding frozen
milk on the doorstep on
a January morning.

Of course, I did not have to test every
tip I came across. Many were simply im-
practical by today's standards—no one
would lavish as much time or effort as the
tip required to salvage an item that, these
days, can be purchased new for a few dollars. We no longer need to save string,
darn the holes in our socks, or paint old,
soiled window shades to make them as
good as new.

But we do have to clean, and most of us
enjoy making our homes as efficient,
comfortable, and comforting as possible.
In this spirit, we offer these tips, culled
from the past and near-present, for your
perusal.

Organization & Clutter Control

How to Clean a Room

Cleaning will be more efficient and effective if you follow these simple rules:

• **HAVE A PLAN.** Don't just say, "I'm going to clean." Be specific. Which room are you going to work on and what will it take to get it cleaned? Does it need just a light dusting and straightening, or will you need to scrub the floors and wash the woodwork? Having a specific list of tasks makes success more likely.

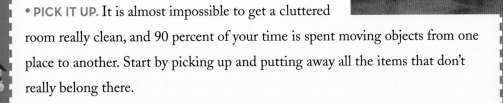

• **PICK IT UP.** It is almost impossible to get a cluttered room really clean, and 90 percent of your time is spent moving objects from one place to another. Start by picking up and putting away all the items that don't really belong there.

The first rule of this household is discipline.

—Christopher Plummer lays down the law as Captain Von Trapp;
The Sound of Music, 1965

• **CLEAN IT ALL.** Whether you're clearing a cluttered desk or an entire room, don't stop when it's "better" or "mostly done." If you do, it will still look cluttered, and as everyone knows, clutter begets more clutter. It's better to do a thorough job on a small area than an incomplete job on a larger area.

• **CLEAN TOP TO BOTTOM.** Start by dusting cobwebs, ceiling fans, cornices, and cupboard tops and work downward, letting the dust fall beneath you, and ending with floors, baseboards, and rugs.

• **DO ONE THING EXTRA.** If you're cleaning a room, do one thing that isn't an absolute must. For example, if you're working in the bathroom, straighten the medicine cabinet one week and the linen closet the next. This way, you will never have a room

that's so out of control the mere thought of cleaning it is overwhelming.

• **LOAD UP.** Figure out which cleaning tools and products you'll be using and carry them with you in a bucket or basket so you won't have to interrupt your cleaning by searching for them.

• **LET CLEANING PRODUCTS SUPPLY THE ELBOW GREASE.** When you're in high-energy cleaning mode, the tendency is to spray surfaces with cleaner and start wiping immediately. However, most household cleaners are more effective if they have a few minutes to work, so spray counters and other surfaces first, find another task to do for a few minutes, *then* come back and start wiping the surface.

• **JUST SAY "NO" TO DISTRACTION.** Monitor your answering machine while cleaning and only pick up for emergencies. And the tempting stack of magazines you'd just *love* to browse through before sending them to the recycling bin?

Set them aside for later. Having a radio or music on can be a good energizer, but leave the TV off—the temptation to watch is just too great.

Need more storage space? *First* do a walk-through of your home, noting where you have unused space and taking precise measurements. Make a plan, *then* go to the container store. Buying storage bins on impulse and hoping they'll fit in somewhere creates more problems than it solves, and storage comes in so many shapes and sizes these days, you can buy exactly what works for you.

Almost every home has an unused niche where a small desk can be set up. A lamp is all that need show on the surface—

everything else, including stationery, stamps, pens, and even a laptop, can be stored in the desk's drawers. Having an extra desk will eliminate the clutter that accumulates on kitchen and dining-room tables when they're used as study areas.

When buying storage containers, whether for the coat closet or the refrigerator, choose square or rectangular units rather than round ones—rectangular containers are much easier to stack, are less likely to tip over, and give you more storage capacity for the space they take up. Storage in a round 14-by-6-inch hatbox: 924 cubic inches; storage in a 14-by-14-by-6-inch square box: 1,176 cubic inches.

"*Quick cleaning with safety*... that's what I want from my cleanser!"

If you live in a two-story home, keep a basket at the top and at the bottom of the stairs to drop off items that need to go to the other floor.

Buy a headset for your cordless phone and use it. You'll be surprised how many necessary little tasks—such as dusting, straightening a drawer, and folding laundry—you can get done.

Don't buy CD or DVD racks with slots—whether you arrange alphabetically or by category, you will have to shift your whole collection every time you want to make space for a new addition. And where will you put the boxed sets?

If you buy wine or liquor by the case, save the empty box with the dividers intact. It makes an ideal storage unit for Christmas ornaments wrapped in tissue, rolled-up posters and gift wrap, or fine but infrequently used crystal goblets.

Use an empty paper towel core to make next year's holiday decorating easier. Wrap holiday lights around the tube, anchoring one end to the bottom and ending with the other at the top. Next season you'll be able to "unreel" without tangles.

Plastic ice cube trays make excellent and inexpensive organizers for desks, utility drawers, and even jewelry drawers. The compartments are just the right size for paper clips, rubber bands, stamps, earrings, rings, and other small items.

Have plenty of wastebaskets, and make sure they are large enough to be useful rather than decorative. Line them with plastic bags for quick, efficient emptying that doesn't scatter dust and debris.

Whenever you buy something new, write the warranty expiration date on the instruction manual and file it away. Go through your file once a year to weed out manuals for items you no longer have.

Whenever you buy something new that will need regular replacement parts—such as a printer that will need ink cartridges or a cordless phone that will need batteries—write the model number and, if specified, the number of the part needed in a small, purse-sized notebook.

Hold Everything:
that's what LANE chests do!

ress by
McCardell

Console in blond oak with superb sculptured Swedish modern base. Note that this Lane stands well off the floor—gives you *cleaning* space too. It's table-height—so the top area is added *decorator* space. Polished brass pulls, and tambour-effect on panelled doors. Inside dimensions hold folded blankets with no waste space. Has deluxe sliding tray midway in cabinet. As shown, in blond oak, C-164. Also comes in pumice-gray finished Walnut, C-165; or in soft-toned American Walnut, C-166.

It will save a lot of searching when the part is needed.

Magazines can quickly grow into large, insurmountable stacks. If you don't have time to read articles when the magazine is current, or if there are articles you want to save, tear them out and throw the rest of the magazine into the recycling bin. Create a filing system for your saved articles, such as "Decorating Ideas," "Recipes," "Crafts," "To Read," etc.

A good way to free up space is to go through your bookshelves often. You'll probably find a lot of outdated reference books that can be tossed for good, because the same information is now available on the Internet.

Designate one place for library books and videos, and keep them there, no matter what room you read or watch videos in. This will avoid frantic last-minute searches and eliminate fines for forgotten items.

If you're doing a major clean-out and know you'll be throwing out a good deal of furniture, lamps, dishes, or other items in good, usable condition, contact a charity and see what their policy is—many will come pick it up at your convenience. Don't overlook churches, community groups, and other nonprofit organizations who often hold annual sales.

Don't be a couch potato. Instead of sitting through commercials, clean during them. You'll get some exercise and salvage 20 minutes of cleaning time for every hour of commercial television. Or record your show, clean for 20 minutes, and watch it as a reward, fast-forwarding through all the commercials.

Keep a project basket in the TV room, and stock it with small, easy-to-pick-up-and-put-down tasks such as mending, correspondence, or magazines and catalogues that need to be looked at.

When you store seldom-used items away, chances are you'll forget what's in the box, so be sure to label the box with its contents.

Keep your family's most important records and phone numbers in a portable file box. If you ever have to leave due to natural disaster, etc., you'll probably have time to take the file box with you.

If you've recently reorganized your storage system, or are in the habit of tucking things away in unusual places to make the most of space, keep a computer or file-card list of reminders on what to find where. It will save you a lot of fruitless searching.

Buy a small notebook and assign a page to each person in your life to whom you give gifts. Whenever an idea comes to you, or the person mentions something they'd like, write it down. This will allow you to avoid the deadly pressure of last-minute shopping, give gifts you're excited about, and save money by taking advantage of sales and specials.

Cake or Powder
whichever you prefer

Bon Ami

for Aluminum etc.

See how it shines! I would never think of using anything but Bon Ami on the *polished* parts of my aluminum ware. It always looks like new because Bon Ami cleans it gently—without the tiniest scratch to mar the polish.

Apply Bon Ami with a wet cloth. A moment's pause while it dries and dissolves the tarnish. Then a dry cloth—away goes the grime—back comes the shine.

Bon Ami is used for cleaning and polishing many things. Look over the list at the right and make sure you are getting all the help that this "good friend" can give you.

THE BON AMI COMPANY, NEW YORK

Principal uses of Bon Ami—
for cleaning and polishing

Bathtubs	Windows
Fine Kitchen Utensils	Mirrors
White Woodwork	Tiling
Aluminum Ware	White Shoes
Brass, Copper and	The Hands
Nickel Ware	Linoleum and
Glass Baking Dishes	Congoleum

"Hasn't Scratched Yet"

A SENSATION!
NEW WHITE OXYDO

washes clothes whiter than ever before!

OXYDOL

NEW! IMPROVED! WHITE OXYDOL!

A WHITER, WHITER SOAP FOR A WHITER, WHITER WASH

Whitest, brightest Oxydol washes ever—
Even when dried inside!

Yes, Oxydol, one of the whitest washing soaps in history has now smashed all its amazing whiteness records!

It's a new *whiter* wash . . . that you can see with your own eyes—instantly. Yes! A whiter white, even when you dry your wash *inside*.

With this new white Oxydol you

get the whitest Oxydol wash you ever had!

And new white Oxydol is truly safe . . . washable colors actually come out brighter.

What's more . . . as long as you use new *white* Oxydol your clothes will keep this new whiteness for

Washing & Ironing

Before putting clothes into the washer:
- Make sure items are right side out and that sleeves and pant legs aren't tangled.
- Set aside ripped items and mend first to prevent further tears.
- Check for and treat stains.
- Empty pockets and close zippers.

To keep garments from discoloring, soak in salt water for 10 minutes before you wash them, or add a dash of vinegar to the wash cycle.

Simply soaking clothes in plain water overnight will go a long way toward getting stains out.

Don't add fabric softener to the water you wash your towels in—it can diminish their absorbency. If your towels have already suffered this fate, bring them back to life by adding a cup of distilled vinegar to the rinse cycle.

If you have a hard time rinsing the suds from your hand washing, add a few tablespoons of vinegar to the first rinse.

Cotton whites will stay whiter if you launder them in cold water and add a spoonful of cream of tartar (available in the spice aisle of the grocery store) to the wash water.

If you have antique linens that are thin from use and age, add starch to the rinse water when you launder them. It will strengthen the fabric and make them look newer.

Even your washer should be washed occasionally to control soap buildup. To clean, run an empty cycle of warm water to which you have added a gallon of vinegar.

To prevent hand-washed sweaters and knitwear from stretching, place them in a colander and gently press out excess moisture before you lay them out to dry.

Save time matching up socks—keep a jar of safety pins by the washing machine and pin pairs together before they go into the wash.

A general rule for stain removal: always work from the outer edges in, toward the center of the stain. Most people instinctively start from the center, where the stain is deepest, but working this way can actually cause the stain to spread.

No spot remover on hand? A good emergency stand-in is a solution of 2 parts water to 1 part isopropyl alcohol.

Soiled collars aren't caused by dirty necks

but by body oils that attract dirt. To clean them, you have to attack the oil. There are two ways to do this. Either rub some shampoo into the collar before washing, or make a paste of vinegar and baking soda, rub on, and wash as usual.

Vinegar is a must for hand washing. Add a little to your rinse water, and it will help remove suds.

Save money by replacing fabric softener with vinegar. A cup added to the rinse cycle will make fabrics soft and fresh.

Garments of lace and other delicate fabrics should be placed in a mesh bag or pillow case for washing to prevent rips and tears.

Quick Stain-Removal Guide

BLOOD: Rinse in cold water as soon as possible. Pour a little hydrogen peroxide directly onto the stain and wash immediately.

CANDLE WAX: Peel off hardened wax. Warm carbon tetrachloride by setting the bottle in a bowl of warm water. (Do

1. NO SOAP CAN BEAT DUZ FOR GETTING TOWELS **WHITE!** NO SOAP GETS WHITE THINGS WHITER!

2. NO SOAP CAN BEAT DUZ FOR GETTING OUT DIRT! DUZ DOES EVEN THE GRIMIEST OVERALLS **CLEAN!**

3. YET DUZ DOES EVEN DAINTY RAYON UNDIES **SAFER** THAN ANY OTHER LEADING WASHDAY PACKAGE SOAP!

NOT heat on the stove or over a flame.) Place a towel beneath the stain and dab with the warmed carbon tetrachloride.

EGG: Soak in cold water, then wash in tepid water until the stain is completely out. Hot water will make the stain set.

GREASE: Make a paste of cornstarch and water and apply to the wrong side of the fabric. Let paste dry, then brush off.

GUM: Place item in freezer long enough for gum to become brittle. Peel off as much of the gum as possible, then apply either carbon tetrachloride or amyl acetate. This should allow you to remove remaining bits with a butter knife or your fingernail.

SPOT-REMOVING SOLVENT (KEEP STOPPERED)

PAD OR BLOTTER

RUB ONE DIRECTION AS INDICATED

Speers

INK FROM A BALLPOINT PEN: Moisten a cotton ball or pad with isopropyl alcohol. Rub until the stain disappears and rinse thoroughly with tepid water.

IRON RUST MARKS: Dampen spots and rub well with cream of tartar (available in the spice aisle of the grocery store). Let stand for an hour, then wash. If some spots still remain, repeat the process.

KETCHUP: Immediately wipe as much of the ketchup away as possible, then flush with a strong concentration of water and detergent. If stains remain, work some glycerin into the fabric, then wash again with the detergent and water solution.

OIL: Dip a wedge of lime in salt, rub the area, then wash.

PAINT: Oil-based paint can be removed from cotton or silk, even if it has set. Pour a generous amount of vinegar in a saucepan and heat. While waiting for the vinegar, position the stained area of the garment over a bowl. When the vinegar reaches the boiling point, pour over the stains. The paint will dissolve without harming the cloth.

RUST: Bring water to a boil in a teakettle. Wet the spot with lemon juice and hold directly over the steam coming from the kettle.

WINE: Wine stains can be removed from linens or cotton by dipping the stained area into boiling milk. Keep the milk at a boil and keep dipping until the stain is completely gone, then rinse and wash.

Clothes will last longer and colors stay brighter if you reduce the dryer heat and dry for a longer period of time, rather than trying to dry them as fast as you can.

If you overload your dryer, clothes won't tumble properly. Not only will it take longer to dry them, but they will wrinkle more.

Removing items from the dryer before they are bone-dry will reduce static cling.

Removing and folding linens while they are still warm will eliminate wrinkles. This is an especially good tip for high-thread-count cotton sheets, which may otherwise need to be ironed.

The greatest laundry-folding challenge ever invented is the fitted sheet. To fold one with ease, fit one corner over your fist, right side up. Now fit either of the adjacent corners inside out over the first corner, so that the right-side seams are together. As you do this, smooth the turned sheet edges so they lie flat. Repeat the same process with the other end of the sheet. You now have a reasonably flat bundle that can be folded tidily without creating new wrinkles.

When putting sheets and towels away, put the freshly laundered ones at the bottom of the stack—your linens will get even use, and you'll never be unpleasantly surprised by stale, dusty linens that have gone unused for far too long.

If you line-dry outdoors, turning clothes inside out will keep them from fading.

Use an old umbrella for a quick, collapsible indoor "clothesline" for lingerie and other lightweight items. Just remove the fabric and hook the handle over the shower rod. An average umbrella with eight ribs of 24 inches each will give you 16 feet of clothesline.

Love your spandex knits? Prolong their life by keeping them out of the dryer. The fibers that make knits stretchy are easily heat-damaged and will retain their resilience longer if they air-dry.

Ironing: Get the Settings Right

ACETATE: cool

ACRYLIC: cool

ALPACA: medium; use steam and iron inside out for best results

CAMEL: medium; use steam and iron inside out for best results

CASHMERE: medium; use steam and iron inside out for best results

COTTON: medium to high; use steam for best results

THE IRON

The gadget we call an iron has been around since the 1600s, and in very much the same form as we know it today. The improvements, however, have been surprisingly recent. The first electric irons were invented in the early twentieth century, but most people didn't have electricity until many years later. Flat irons that heated on the stove—or more dangerous models that contained kerosene, acetylene, and even gasoline—were used in some areas until World War II. Controllable heat settings didn't appear until the 1920s, and today's big feature—steam—wasn't common until the 1950s. Many of today's adults remember when Mom kept a sprinkling bottle at hand to dampen each item before pressing. All things considered, today's ironing should be a snap. It isn't, for one simple reason: most of us, dazzled by the promise of a wrinkle-free, permanent-press world, never learned how to iron in the first place!

LINEN: medium to high; use steam for best results

LYCRA: cool to medium

MOHAIR: medium; use steam and iron inside out for best results

NYLON: low

POLYESTER: low to medium

RAMIE: medium to high; use steam for best results

RAYON: low; iron inside out for best results

SILK: low; iron inside out for best results

WOOL: medium; use steam and iron inside out for best results

To iron a shirt, blouse, jacket or blazer, follow this order:
- Trimmings
- Underside of collar
- Upper side of collar
- Back side of sleeves and cuffs
- Front side of sleeves and cuffs
- Back of garment
- Front inner facings
- Front of garment

If ironing a dress, do the bodice first and the skirt last.

To iron slacks, iron the pockets first, then the waistband, then the derriere and front down to the crotchline. Next, lay both legs out, overlapping, with the inseams aligned and the legs smooth, straight and matching. Peel the top leg back and iron the inseam side of the bottom leg, moving from the seam out and straightening as you go to create perfect, sharp creases down the front and back of the leg. Flip pants over and repeat with the second leg. Now bring the inseams together and iron the upper (side-seam) side of each leg. Immediately hang the pants up or let them cool completely on a flat surface. Never lay freshly ironed pants over the back of a chair—you'll create new creases.

If you have several items to iron, start with those that need the coolest setting, and progress to those that need higher temperatures.

Let your freshly ironed clothes cool completely before wearing or hanging in the closet—it's the cooling process that sets the pressing.

Ironing will be much less of a chore if you hang up or fold items as soon as they come out of the dryer. Most wrinkles form when warm clothes sit in a heap, waiting for ironing day.

Shiny iron marks? Ironing from the wrong side or using a pressing cloth will put a stop to that.

Makers of fine Irish table linens tell us that placing the items in a plastic bag and refrigerating them 6 to 24 hours beforehand will make them much easier to iron.

Folding fine linens the same way every time will create wear marks in the fabric. To avoid this, alternate folding methods, such as folding in thirds one time and in quarters the next.

To get a smooth finish and protect delicate buttons on a garment, use a spoon. Invert the tip of the spoon over the button and use it to both shield and angle the button— you'll be easily able to iron the area that is under the button without causing any harm.

Before you iron, go over your ironing board with a lint brush or slightly damp cloth—your clothes won't pick up any stray pet hairs, lint, or other bits of debris.

There's a reason ironing boards are adjustable. If you have a lot of pieces to do, adjust the board to table height, pull up a chair, and relax.

If ironed embroidery or eyelet fabric comes out looking flattened or puckered, lay a terry cloth towel on your ironing board, turn the fabric face down, and iron from the wrong side.

To give a necktie a professionally ironed look, cut a cardboard template to fit inside, cover the tie with a handkerchief, use steam, and press lightly.

To iron a dress or skirt cut on the bias, iron with the weave of the fabric. Ironing from waist to hem stretches the fabric and, over time, will result in a wavy hemline.

To iron pleats, use paper clips to fasten the pleats at the bottom.

If you use starch, it may collect on your iron. To remove, cut a piece from a brown paper grocery bag, sprinkle with salt, and press with the iron set on hot.

If you scorch something while ironing, immediately dab the spot with a cloth dipped in vinegar or hydrogen peroxide. Rub gently until the scorch marks are gone, then dab with water to rinse out the vinegar and iron dry.

Use distilled water to avoid clogging your steam iron with mineral deposits. If these clogs do occur, here's the remedy:

1. Let the iron cool completely and make sure it is unplugged.

2. Use a bamboo skewer or cotton swab to remove any mineral deposits you see on the bottom of the iron.

3. Use a sewing needle to clear the spray nozzle of the iron.

4. Mix equal parts distilled water and white vinegar. Fill the iron's water reservoir with this.

5. Place a heatproof rack over a sink or metal bowl and set the iron on it, ironing plate down and vents facing down into the bowl or sink. Make sure the vents are not covered.

6. Plug in the iron and choose the steam setting. Let it run until the steam stops.

7. Fill the iron with plain distilled water and let the iron run until the steam stops.

8. Unplug the iron, gently wipe the bottom, and let cool.

Always make sure the bottom of the iron is dry before putting it away. This will prevent clogs and rust spots in the future.

Stevan Dohanos

Satin
IMPERVO
Low Lustre Enamel
WHITE

Walls, Windows & Doors

To remove a grease spot from wallpaper, act fast. Mix cornstarch with water to make a thick paste. Dab it onto the stain, let dry completely, then brush away. If the grease spot has not set for too long, the paste should absorb the grease.

To remove crayon marks from wallpaper, try the method above.

Scotch tape on wallpaper can stain the wallpaper beneath if left on. To remove it without tearing the wallpaper, cover with a towel and press with a warm iron. The warmth should loosen the adhesive enough to let you peel the tape away.

Light marks and smudges on wallpaper can often be removed with a gum eraser. Rub gently—if the mark isn't going to come off, rubbing harder won't help, and you don't want to risk marring your wallpaper.

Paint rooms that get heavy use—such as kitchens and children's bedrooms—with semigloss rather than flat paint. Semigloss is less likely to show marks as clearly and is easier to clean.

Tips for splatter-free painting with a brush:

1. Don't dip the brush too deeply into the paint.

2. Don't finish each stroke with a flourish. It's fun, but flipping the brush scatters droplets all over.

3. As you stroke, paint is automatically pushed toward the base of the brush,

where it accumulates. To keep it from dripping, stroke outwards from time to time.

4. Hold the handle close to the brush head, not at the end. It's the lever principle at work—the longer the lever, the wider the arc of swing, and the harder to control.

Tips for splatter-free painting with a roller:

1. Don't dip the roller too deeply. In fact, don't dip the roller into the paint reservoir much at all—just enough to bring some paint up onto the slanted part of the tray—and load your roller from there.

2. Work the paint into the roller. Roll the roller back and forth several times, pressing firmly, to make the roller grip the paint. Paint that merely sits on the surface of the roller will drip, splatter, and go on in thick, uneven streaks.

3. Roll slowly. Fast rolling will produce an unfortunate spin-art effect.

4. Put your shoulders into it. Don't just swipe the roller back and forth. Really press as you go, working the paint in for even coverage. This is especially important for ceilings.

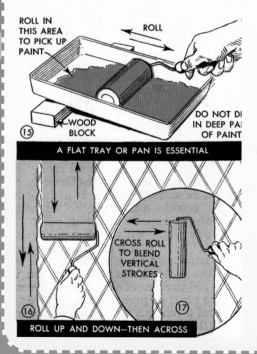

ROLL IN THIS AREA TO PICK UP PAINT

ROLL

WOOD BLOCK

DO NOT DI IN DEEP PAI OF PAINT

(15)

A FLAT TRAY OR PAN IS ESSENTIAL

CROSS ROLL TO BLEND VERTICAL STROKES

(16)

(17)

ROLL UP AND DOWN—THEN ACROSS

You can do such wonderful things with color!

Super Kem-Tone®

THE DELUXE WASHABLE WALL PAINT

Before you put the leftover paint away, cut a piece of cardboard or posterboard the size of a piece of an 8½ x 11 paper and give it two or three coats. When it's dry, file it away. When you shop for new items for the room, take it along—it will give you a much better idea of how things will coordinate than the small sample on a paint card.

Give freshly painted walls a thin coating of spray starch. It will protect the paint and make the walls easier to clean; when it wears off you can easily reapply it.

When you've finished painting your walls and want to get rid of the fumes fast, place several charcoal briquets in a pan, leave in the center of the room, and close the doors for several hours.

Keep leftover paint fresh and ready for touch-ups. Instead of leaving it in the no-longer-airtight can, pour it into a clean, dry plastic milk or laundry jug. Don't forget to add a label identifying the paint by manufacturer, color, number, and storage date.

Make an inexpensive, and perfectly effective, window-cleaning solution by adding 2 or 3 tablespoons of vinegar or ammonia (but not both) to a gallon of cool water.

To clean windows, buy a rubber-edged squeegee. Squeegees work faster and better than spray and paper towels, can be bought in almost any hardware store, and aren't even expensive, especially when you consider the paper towels you'll be saving. Squeegees come in a variety of widths, some have curved edges for hard-to-reach places, and many can be fitted onto extender poles. It's the best gadget most people don't buy.

The best time to wash windows is on a cloudy day when no rain is threatened, or late in the day when the sunlight is weak. The reason? Direct sunlight can dry the cleaning solution before you have time to wipe it off, and this causes streaks.

Save on paper towels, too: unbelievable as it sounds, newspaper cleans windows just as well and will leave them virtually lint-free.

For spot-cleaning windows, try a little isopropyl alcohol.

If you have intricate windows with small panes, dip a cotton swab in cleaning solution to reach into the corners.

Discolored spots on aluminum window frames are usually caused by oxidation. To remove them, try a mildly abrasive powdered cleanser or liquid detergent.

You can prevent oxidation spots from forming on aluminum window frames by cleaning first, then applying auto paste wax. Repeat the application once a year.

CEILING
TAPE
⑦

1-INCH WIDE MASKING TAPE IS EXCELLENT FOR OB-TAINING BORDER EFFECTS

⑥

MIX WATER PAINT WITH YOUR HANDS—IT WASHES OFF EASILY (SEE TABLE No. 2)

⑧

Bon Ami —*makes cleaning time playtime!*

"HERE'S our little Bon Ami Chick, just like the one we read about in your Ami Fairy Booklet."

ow then—one whisk and away goes tle Chick . . . . all the dust . . . . all reaks and the spatters. In two jiffs, indow will be so clear, we'll have to wice to make sure the glass didn't ay too!"

n Ami *Cake*, America's favorite w and mirror cleaner for thirty-ears, is today more popular than Every woman knows how quickly and easily it cleans and polishes.

for bathtub, basin and tiling

"Hasn't Scratched Yet"

POWDER AND CAKE

every home needs both

Rub it on with a damp cloth . . . . in a moment it's dry . . . . then wipe it off with a clean, dry cloth. Simplest, safest way in the world to make windows and mirrors clear and bright!

FOR some uses, you'll find the *Powder* form of Bon Ami very convenient. You'll like the way the soft scratchless powder polishes up the bathtub, sweetens the refrigerator, cleans the kitchen sink and painted woodwork, removes every spot from Congoleum floor-coverings, etc.

There are dozens of uses in every house for both Bon Ami *Powder* and Bon Ami *Cake*. They blot up dirt—never scratch —keep your hands smooth and soft. It's so convenient to have these "Partners in Cleanliness" on hand all the time.

THE BON AMI COMPANY . . . . . NEW YORK
In Canada—BON AMI LIMITED, MONTREAL

A Fairy Tale for the Children!

The story of the beautiful Princess Bon Ami, her gallant Bunny Knights and their wonderful trip to the foot of the rainbow. Written in amusing rhyme with many illustrations, this beautifully colored book will bring fun to the youngsters. Send 4 cents in stamps for your copy. Address The Bon Ami Co., 10 Battery Place, New York, N. Y.

NAME

ADDRESS

CITY

Do you use Bon Ami? (*Powder* ☐ *Cake* ☐ *Both* ☐)

Your goal: Try to make sure your home is a place of peace, order, and tranquility . . .

—"The Good Wife's Guide," *Housekeeping Monthly*, May 13, 1955

When you wash windows inside and out, use vertical strokes on one side and horizontal strokes on the other. This way, you'll know at once which side any streaks are on.

A small hole in a screen can be repaired by dabbing it with a bit of model airplane glue. When the glue dries, the mend will be barely visible.

Large holes in screens can be fixed by cutting a patch from an old screen or from purchased screen mesh and gluing the patch over the hole.

If frost forms on your windows in the cold months, you may have your humidifier set too high.

If frost forms on windows due to poor window construction or insulation, polishing the insides of the panes with isopropyl alcohol will help.

Have trouble remembering which curtain or drape goes on which window when you take them down for washing or cleaning? Use the rainbow system. Go around the room and assign each window a color in the order of the rainbow: red, orange, yellow, green, blue, indigo, and violet. Then stitch and knot a matching loop of thread in each curtain before you take them down. When they're back in place, just snip and remove the thread.

To make freshly washed curtains hang evenly, thread a curtain rod through the bottom hem overnight. Not only will your curtains hang evenly, but they won't develop crimps or wrinkles.

Curtains and drapes can help conserve energy and keep a room warm in winter. Choose light-colored fabrics over darker ones, since they will allow sunlight into the room, rather than blocking it.

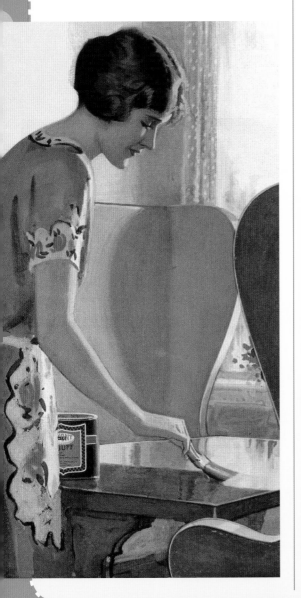

Curtains and drapes that are lined will also help by holding warmth in the room.

For maximum help with temperature control, have two sets of drapes and curtains, one for summer and one for winter. The summer set should be light and sheer, while the winter set should be of heavier fabric and, preferably, lined.

When trying to position tie-backs so they are even on both sides, lower the blinds and use the horizontal edge as your guide.

If a door hangs unevenly and one edge scrapes along the floor, tightening the screws in the hinges should bring it back into line.

Squeaking door hinges can be silenced with vegetable cooking spray. Spray directly onto the hinge, open and close the door several times to let the spray work in, then wipe off any excess.

Your New Hoover

"Easy Cleaning" is its middle name!

Rolls like a doll buggy.

Keeps rug colors fresh.

Picks up dog hairs and lint in a jiffy.

No stooping or straining because the Hoover "stands up to you."

Easy to get out — easy to put away.

Never before so much Hoover at so low a price.

Converts instantly, with a simple push of the hand, from rug cleaner to easy-to-use cleaner for draperies, upholstery, lamp shades, bare floors and linoleum.

THE HOOVER
REG. U. S. PAT. OFF

It beats . . . as it sweeps . . . as it cleans

THE HOOVER COMPANY, NORTH CANTON, OHIO
HAMILTON, ONTARIO, CANADA

The Army-Navy "E" award
received four times for high
achievement in the production

Floors & Floor Coverings

The easiest way to cut down on floor and carpet grime is to keep it out of your house in the first place. Employ a two-doormat system at each door, placing one mat outside the door and a second one inside. People will automatically wipe their feet twice, and the amount of dirt you'll find on the inside mat is proof positive of the system's efficiency.

In bad weather, line a rectangular, flat-bottomed box or basket with paper for wet shoes and boots. It will keep mud and grit from getting tracked across your floors. Keeping a cozy basket of slippers and warm, dry socks nearby will up compliance.

If you have hardwood, tile, or linoleum floors, sweeping puts almost as much dust back in the air as it gathers up. Consider using a dry mop or vacuum.

Make sweeping more efficient by dampening the ends of your broom. If you dampen the edge of your dustpan as well, it will keep the sweepings from rolling back onto the floor.

MODERN KITCHENS REQUIRE PARTICULAR FLOORS

Don't neglect to clean the broom. Run cool water over it to wash out dust and debris. When it is really dirty, let the broom head soak in a bucket of cool water for 20–30 minutes. If your broom is made of natural straw, the water will lengthen the life of the broom by keeping it pliable.

Water is hard on wood floors, so wash them as infrequently as possible.

The best method for everyday cleaning is to vacuum them.

To prevent furniture from scratching or marking your floors when you move it, put sweat socks over the legs first.

Try this remedy for creaky floorboards: rub talcum powder into the cracks, then wipe away the excess.

Wooden rockers on a hardwood floor can quickly ruin the floor's finish, as well as the rocker's. To protect all of your wood, cover the bottom of each rocker with a strip of masking tape.

Another way to protect floors from wooden rockers is to wax the bottom of the rockers when you wax your floors.

To remove rubber shoe marks, try an ordinary eraser.

What to do if nail polish spills on a hard-surface floor? If it is just a small drop, wipe it up immediately. If the spill is larger, wiping it up will create a large smear. In this case, allow the polish to almost set. When it has congealed but is still pliable, use the edge of a butter knife to lift one edge, then peel the spill up. Once the polish has completely set, only a solvent will loosen it.

If your child makes crayon marks on your vinyl floor, rubbing with a bit of silver polish should erase them.

Make a disposable mop head without spending the money. Just cut one leg from a pair of ruined panty hose, slide it over your regular dust mop, and secure it by tying it into place. When you've finished dusting, remove it by peeling the stocking down—inside out, to trap the dust—and throw it away.

If a corner of vinyl tile or linoleum has come loose, ask for the appropriate glue at your hardware store. Spread glue on a butter knife, gently slide the knife under the loose corner, and withdraw the knife while pressing the loose floor covering down against it to thoroughly "butter" the underside. Press the corner firmly into place, wipe up any seeping glue, cover with a sheet of plain white paper, and weight down with a flat, heavy object, such as a stack of books. Leave in place for a full day to make sure the repaired area is not disturbed.

To give your waxed floors a quick touch-up, go over them with a piece of waxed paper. Not only will this renew the wax, but it will also pick up bits of dust and grit that dry mopping might miss. Refold or replace the paper when it becomes soiled and the wax has been rubbed off.

No rugs or carpets, they're just dust collectors . . . Linoleum through the whole house, wait until you see the pictures, it's sleek and smooth, easy to keep clean . . . It's like every room in the house was a bathroom!

—State Fair, 1945

When the felt pads on a floor polisher are stiff with old wax, you can get more use from them by placing them between several sheets of newspaper and going over them with a hot iron. A good deal of the wax will melt into the paper. Replace the paper if the inner layers become saturated, and be careful not to let it soak through onto your iron or ironing board.

Cut down on vacuuming, sweeping, and scrubbing floors by instituting a "no shoes indoors" policy. Most of the dirt and dust that soils the floor comes in on the bottoms of shoes and boots.

Fringe is usually the first part of a rug to wear out. If the rug isn't expensive enough to have professionally repaired, trim away the fringe and cover the edges with the wide fabric binding tape used for finishing hooked rugs. The tape, available in crafts stores, can be sewn on or attached with a glue gun.

The outer edge of a braided rug needs protection to keep from wearing out too soon. When the rug is still new, attach carpet or binding tape around the outer edge on the underside of the rug, positioning it so the edge comes a fraction of the way up the side but isn't visible from above. If the braid is already worn, cover the edge completely with binding tape, as described for a fringed rug, above.

When you buy a large area rug or have carpeting installed, be sure to record vital information such as the manufacturer's name, model number, fiber content, and grade. Not only will this help the dealer address any questions you might have down the road, but it will help professional cleaners know how to treat stains that need attention.

The best way to rid carpeting or rugs of odors is with a substance called zeolite, also known as "volcanic mineral" because it's a form of volcanic rock. It's safe and non-toxic to animals, plants, and humans, and can usually be found in pet or swimming-pool supply stores. It comes in powder or crystal form; follow the package directions for best results. Zeolite works by absorbing the odor directly from the carpet and after use can be swept up, left in the sun to deodorize, and used again. It can also be used on upholstery.

If new runners are being installed in a stairway, have extra length cut equal to

CAVALCADE OF PROGRESS

1902 *Popular Mechanics* magazine sets off a century-long handyman frenzy

Waldorf toilet paper

1903 Wire hangers patented

1908 Hoover electric vacuum cleaner, with bag and attachments

1911 GE electric waffle iron

1914 Kelvinator refrigerator

1920 Brillo

Frigidaire refrigerator

1921 Drano

Electrolux vacuum cleaner

1932 Johnson's Glo-Coat floor wax

1933 Windex

1937 InSinkErator garbage disposal

1939 Electric carving knife

1941 Vinyl furniture

1946 Tupperware!

1947 Ajax powdered cleanser

GE two-door refrigerator-freezer

Reynolds Wrap aluminum foil

Sears Kenmore top-loading automatic washer

1950 CorningWare — from oven to table to freezer

Yes, Frigidaire, the electrical home refrigerator, actually freezes your own favorite drinking water into cubes for table use.

—Frigidaire ad, 1921

1922 Maytag Gyrofoam washing machine

1924 *Better Homes and Gardens* magazine

1926 Toastmaster pop-up electric toaster

1927 GE Monitor Top refrigerator

Cheese slicer

1929 Gas stove

1930 GE room air conditioner

Sunbeam Mixmaster

1931 Scott paper towels and napkins

Spic-n-Span detergent

1951 Push-button garage door opener

1953 Saran Wrap

Sunbeam Electric Skillet

1954 GE combination washer/dryer

Weber grill

1956 Comet cleanser

GE toaster oven

1957 Pastel toilet paper

1958 Mr. Clean cleanser

1963 GE self-cleaning oven

the height of a riser. Install the runner with the extra length folded under on the bottom riser. Then, when the covering on the steps shows wear, you can lift up the runner, unfold the extra length so that it covers the bottom riser, and move everything up accordingly. The parts of the runner that were on the steps will now cover the risers, while the unworn parts on the risers will now cover the steps.

Prolong the life of area rugs by turning them end to end regularly so they will wear evenly, without showing traffic patterns.

Vacuum the padding beneath an area rug at least twice a year. Not only is this important for eliminating dust, but vacuuming will plump the padding and provide a fuller base for the rug.

To remedy a rug that curls at the corner, fold the corner over in the opposite direction and press down firmly with a warm iron for a few minutes. Unfold, and weight down with a book for an hour or two.

Antique or delicate rugs should be rolled with the right side out to avoid compacting the pile.

When moving furniture, never drag it across carpeting or rugs—the tugging could pull and damage the pile.

To remedy the dents furniture puts in your carpet, dampen a cloth, lay it over the depression, and press with a hot iron. (Do not let the iron come into direct

contact with the carpeting, which may contain synthetic fibers that can melt or fuse.) After you've removed the cloth, gently brush the carpet to plump it up.

Clip loose strands that protrude above the surface of a carpet or rug with scissors to avoid snagging. Never pull at them, which may damage the weave.

Sprinkle carpet and large rugs with salt occasionally before you vacuum. The salt will pick up extra dust and discourage carpet moths.

A freshly cleaned carpet should be allowed to dry completely before you place furniture on it, to avoid making dents. If this isn't possible, buy coasters at a hardware store and place one under each leg. Position the furniture a few inches to the left or right of where you want it to end up. When the carpet is completely dry, remove the coasters, move the furniture into its permanent position, and gently fluff up any dents left by the coasters.

The chemicals in some furniture polishes can cause alterations in color if they interact with carpet dyes. To keep this from happening, slide a brown paper bag or several sheets of newspaper under the piece of furniture you're polishing.

If hot candle wax spills onto your carpet, try to remove as much as possible before it hardens. To do this, lay a brown paper bag over the spill and apply an iron set on medium (don't use steam). A good deal of the wax will be absorbed by the paper.

General Guidelines For Removing Stains From Carpets and Rugs

Know the fiber content and the manufacturer's care instructions before you begin. Some carpets are specially treated and may be damaged by conventional cleaning methods.

Use plain white towels or paper towels when blotting stains, as stain removers may cause colors to run.

Start with the mildest solution first, and only move on to something stronger if necessary.

Blot toward the center. Be careful not to widen the stain by pushing the spilled material outward.

No matter what product you use, or how well it works, be sure to rinse it all out of the carpet after you've finished. The same molecules that magically bond with the stain will go right on attracting more than their share of dirt and grease, and the spot you just cleaned will become soiled more quickly if the substance is not removed.

Family Room & Living Room

An easy way to avoid costly decorating mistakes is to browse home decor magazines, find a room you love, and duplicate the look as your budget allows. You'll end up with something you love, you'll get lots of compliments, and no one will ever know you cheated.

If soot or smoke stains have blemished the exterior of your fireplace and the stains aren't too large, try using a gum eraser to remove them. For larger stained areas, both outside and inside the fireplace, use a scrub brush and a solution of dishwashing liquid and warm water.

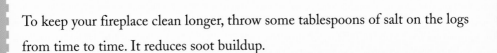

To keep your fireplace clean longer, throw some tablespoons of salt on the logs from time to time. It reduces soot buildup.

Don't throw away your orange and lemon peels. Scrape them clean, let them dry thoroughly, and toss them into your next fire for a sweet, tangy scent.

After trying all sorts of items, from special dusters to the attachment on our vacuum cleaner, we found nothing that cleaned our lampshades faster or better than a felt pad–style lint brush. One or two swipes removed dust, lint, and even stray pet hair.

Parchment or heavy paper lampshades that have become soiled needn't be thrown out. Try a wallpaper cleaner before you give up on them.

Table lamps can be quite expensive, but before you hand over the dough, do some shopping and some math. Many formal lamps get their look of elegance and luxury from the shade, not from the lamp itself. You may be able to buy a far less expensive lamp, splurge on a separate shade, and walk away with money to spare.

When choosing china cabinets, shelves, and other storage furniture, think about the value of doors—they will reduce your dusting immeasurably. Glass doors add elegance in the living and dining rooms. In less formal rooms, solid doors are godsends for hiding clutter in a hurry.

Children like to play wherever the rest of the family is, and this often results in an excess of toys scattered over the family room. For quick pick-up, buy a plastic bin, help the child round up everything at the end of the day, and take the bin along to the bedroom as part of the bedtime routine. The rule: no more toys than the bin can hold.

When dry-dusting the television screen, turn the set on. The light will show any missed spots, and you won't have to go back over it later.

If your pictures don't hang straight, it's often because the wires they hang from are smooth and slip easily. To remedy the situation, wrap masking tape around the center part of each wire (the part that goes over the hook). The slight roughness of the tape will keep your pictures from slipping.

Put a small felt pad or thumbtack on each bottom corner of a picture frame. This will guard against scuffing and prevent a dust line from forming.

Not sure where to hang a new picture or mirror? Trace around it on brown paper, cut out, and use masking tape to tack it to the wall. Now you can step back and see if that's where you really want it. If it is, mark where the hanger should be placed before you take the cutout down.

The easiest way to dust books is with an inexpensive paint brush 2 or 3 inches wide.

A cloth dipped in milk has many uses. It will shine the leaves of potted plants, as well as piano keys and gilt picture frames.

If you use slipcovers, skip the ironing after you wash them. Instead, put them back on while still slightly damp. Make sure they're correctly positioned, smooth them with your hand, and they'll dry smooth and better fitting than if you'd ironed them.

An easy way to discourage your cat from sleeping on the sofa or good chair is to tuck a few mothballs into the cushion. They just don't like the smell.

Carved wood furniture is lovely to look at but can be a challenge to dust and polish. For crevices you can't quite reach, use a cotton swab. A swab dipped in polish is also an excellent way to protect and shine.

The biggest enemy of wood furniture is dry winter air. When you look for ways to keep the environment hydrated, don't forget the green. Houseplants are an attractive and inexpensive way to put moisture in the air.

Dry air is also a threat to leather furniture. A time-honored remedy to prevent cracks and keep leather pliant is an occasional rubdown with a solution of one part vinegar to two parts linseed oil. However, because many of today's leather furnishings have been specially treated, ask the manufacturer or your furniture dealer which products to use.

If caned or rattan furniture becomes very loose, give it a hot shower on a sunny summer day. Thoroughly wet just the parts that are sagging, then carry the piece outside to dry in the sun—the warming rays will shrink the woven strips back into place. When completely dry, apply lemon oil to the entire piece to prevent drying and cracking.

If you decorate with straw or vine baskets, give them a good rinse in the tub every now and then. Not only will the water clean them as ordinary dusting can't, but moistening helps keep the wood from becoming brittle and prone to splitting.

A cigarette burn on wooden furniture mars the entire piece. If the burn is very light, rubbing with a small amount of mayonnaise on a soft cloth may erase it. Larger burns should be attended to by a professional.

Superficial nicks and scratches on wood furniture can often be concealed with ordinary crayons. Go over the spot just enough to hide the flaw, always working in the direction of the grain and blending with another color if necessary to get the right match. Use a soft cloth to work the crayon into the scratch, and your fingernail to gently scrape away any excess.

For deep scratches and nicks in your furniture, or when dealing with an expensive or heirloom piece, you will want the care of a professional. Never try to refinish a spot yourself, as your chances of success are not as great as your chances of failure.

Lemon juice is an excellent cleaner for a glass tabletop.

Clean mirrors to sparkling perfection inexpensively. Wash with water to which a tablespoon of ammonia has been added, and dry with a soft cloth or paper towel. Or, for a lint-free and cost-free alternative, dry with newspaper.

To conceal scratches on a glass tabletop, try rubbing with a bit of toothpaste. If the scratches aren't too deep, this should work.

If grease is spilled on upholstery, cover the spot immediately with cornstarch or talcum powder and let set until as much of the grease as possible has been absorbed. Vacuum up and repeat if necessary.

THE NOT-SO-GOLDEN PAST

Since we're sharing the best classic hints with you, we thought we'd pass along the worst of all time. According to one 1950s era book, an inexpensive way to clean upholstery began with a loaf of bread. We were instructed to cut the loaf in half and use it as an eraser on soiled chair and sofa arms and cushions. All we got was a crumby armchair.

To discourage dust on television and computer screens, wipe with an anti-static dryer sheet.

A dash of baking soda in an ashtray will cut down on cigarette smell.

If artificial flowers brighten your rooms, dusting delicate petals can be difficult. For best results, spray dust away with the same canned compressed air used on computer keyboards. If the flowers have become downright dingy, clean by putting them in a bag with salt and shaking gently for a minute or so. The salt picks up the dirt and dust particles.

Stubborn dust caught in the crevices of artificial flowers and porcelain figurines can be removed with a small watercolor brush.

Nothing is as elegant as candles on the table—until they start to drip. To keep dripping to a minimum, place tapers in the refrigerator for a few hours before you use them. Cold candles also burn longer, so you'll save money as well.

If you use a standing screen to partition off an office area, line the back of the screen with cork or felt so it can double as a bulletin board.

Bedroom

How To Clean a Clothes Closet

Do your efforts to clean the closet end with moving things from one pile to another and, ultimately, putting most of it back where it came from? Stick to these simple guidelines and your efforts will pay off.

IDENTIFY THE PROBLEM. Is your closet just overcrowded? Or so poorly organized you have a hard time finding things? Or do you have plenty of clothes but "nothing to wear" because a large percentage of your wardrobe is out of style, not to your liking, no longer your size, faded and worn, or in need of repair? Your cleaning time will be more productive if you can focus on one or two main problems.

MAKE A PLAN. How are you going to resolve the problem? For most of us, it's a matter of getting rid of the excess and finding additional storage space, so it's a good idea to have goals such as "Reduce wardrobe by 25 percent," or "Move

T-shirts to drawers," or "Hang skirts and slacks on tiered hangers."

GATHER THE NECESSARY ITEMS. Buy new storage bins and hangers *before* you begin. You should also have a good supply of large, strong garbage bags on hand.

MAKE SURE THE REST OF THE ROOM IS CLEAN, WITH PLACES TO SET THINGS. Allocate and label a place for each category of item, such as:

Wearable as is. Return to closet

Save for sentimental reasons. Store in another location, if possible.

Try on. If you haven't worn something for a while, try it on to see if it still looks smart enough to wear.

Wash and mend. Washables go straight to the laundry. Items that need mending should be tagged with the problem to be corrected, such as missing button, undone hem, etc.

Professional attention needed. Depending on what needs to be done, tag each item Clean, Repair, or Alter, and bag them for drop-off.

Discard. It's all right to save a few worn T-shirts to wear for dirty cleaning jobs—

but only a few. The rest have to go.

Pass along to a friend. If you are giving items to more than one friend, have a separate bag for each.

Donate. Yes, donate. If you were going to sell your unworn clothes on eBay, you would have done it already. Be sure to keep a list of the donated items, and have it initialed when you drop the items off, as donated clothes are tax-deductible.

Handle once. This is the hardest, but most effective, rule of all: make sure every garment goes to one of the designated piles. No postponing hard decisions—that's where all those messy, problematic piles that get stuffed back into the closet come from.

The reward for staying tidy is more storage space: if you discipline yourself to hang all of your short garments (such as blouses and blazers) together, you will be able to fit a small chest, cabinet or shoe rack underneath them.

Store your extra scented candles in dresser drawers instead of sachet. Just make sure the candles are wrapped in cellophane or tissue to avoid accidental wax stains.

If you don't like clothes that smell of mothballs (and who can blame you?), try lavender. Either the plant or the oil will work, and the smell is wonderful. The drawback is that it will repel adult moths but won't kill them. So make sure your closet is free of eggs and larvae first.

When you flip your mattress, use the opportunity to vacuum both sides with the upholstery attachment of your vacuum cleaner. It will get rid of a lot of dust and detritus, and discourage dust mites from settling in.

Clothes put away for the season can get stale, dusty, and wrinkled, even if they were put away clean. An inexpensive way to keep them fresh is to cut a hole in the center bottom seam of a large, heavy garbage bag, then invert it over a hanger. Each bag will accommodate several garments.

To reduce humidity in a damp closet, fill a large, empty Cool Whip (or similar) container with charcoal briquets. Punch numerous holes in the lid, snap on and tape securely. Put it on your closet floor and replace charcoal as it becomes soft and crumbly with absorbed moisture.

One-stop clearance: If your children's outgrown clothing might work for your friends' children, drop it off to them and let *them* donate or pass along what they can't use after they've sorted through it.

Gotta straighten out that closet one of these days.

—Jim Jordan, as Fibber McGee, outlines the impossible;
Heavenly Days, 1944

Children are more likely to make their own beds if they don't have to cope with layers of linens. Use an all-in-one duvet system instead of sheet, blanket, and bedspread.

If you want your kids to help keep their rooms clean, avoid lids wherever possible. They're more likely to put toys away in a bin than in a lidded toy chest, and while a clothes hamper might sit empty, kids will willingly toss their dirty clothes into an open basket.

Wash mattress pads at least once a month. Most people don't wash mattress pads often enough—a mistake, as they attract both dust and dust mites, which can aggravate allergies.

To fluff up down pillows and comforters, place them in a clothes dryer on low heat and let them tumble for 10 to 15 minutes.

Need more storage space? Storage bins on rollers, made to slide under the bed, are perfect for clothes that won't be needed until the season changes.

If your clothes slide off their hangers, use clothes pins to clip them in place.

If drawers stick when you pull them, rub a bar of soap over the spots that stick.

A good way to dust blinds is to lower and close them, then brush with a slightly dampened paintbrush (the type made for applying latex paint).

Don't toss out your bedside lamps just

because you've changed color schemes. Give them a good primer coat, then paint them with leftover wall paint.

Launder or dry-clean clothes before storing, as moths and other insects are attracted to grease spots and other food stains.

If you use mothballs, place them as high in the closet as possible, since fumes tend to filter down.

If you don't want to use mothballs, soap slivers tucked between blanket folds, ground black pepper sprinkled on fabric, cotton balls soaked in camphor, blocks of cedar wood, and borax (or borax mixed with powdered sugar) sprinkled on shelves are all good repellents.

Ⓐ
"YIPPEE" WESTERN TWIN SIZE SPREAD 5.98

Ⓑ
"CALANDRA" SWIRL FULL SIZE SPREAD 6.98

Ann said . . . . "Your tub is always so smooth and clean . . . and there's never a bit of gritty sediment in it"

and I said . . . . "Yes, Bon Ami washes away completely . . . . and doesn't it leave a lovely polish !"

★ Bon Ami

"hasn't scratched yet"

If you are using some other cleanser on your bathtub, make this little test. Try one package of Bon Ami—and see how much cleaner *and more lustrous* your tub will look. Notice how Bon Ami *polishes as it cleans* . . . leaving the surface undulled and glistening smooth. Watch how quickly and easily Bon Ami washes away—with no gritty sediment left behind. And you'll enjoy working with Bon Ami. All women do, because it's so white and odorless . . . so gritless—yet so quick and thorough!

Bathroom

Save slivers of soap in a heatproof jar. When the jar is half full, cover slivers with boiling water and stir to make a gel.

Using liquid or glycerin soap in the bath and shower will reduce soap scum buildup.

Dirty grout? Before you use something stronger, try an ordinary pencil eraser.

"Hasn't scratched yet!"

If grout is heavily soiled, apply undiluted vinegar.

For light stains on porcelain tiles, sinks, and tubs, wet the surfaces, then spray with a solution of diluted bleach, mixed by adding ½ cup bleach to 8 cups water.

The best way to keep tiles and tub clean is to keep them free of soap scum in the first place. Get into the habit of rinsing the shower walls or tub immediately

after use, rather than letting residue form. Rinse thoroughly, then finish by rubbing with some lemon. The lemon fights the scum and leaves a fresh scent.

Try rubbing stains on a sink or tub with the cut surface of a lemon. For stains that cannot be removed with lemon, try making a paste of hydrogen peroxide and cream of tartar (available in the spice aisle of the grocery store). Apply the paste, scrub with a non-scratching pad or brush, and rinse thoroughly.

Rust stains on a sink or tub can be especially stubborn. To get rid of them, try a paste of borax and lemon juice, applied with a non-scratching pad or brush. The same paste can be used on the toilet.

Mold that forms on grout and other hard surfaces can be cleaned with a solution of 3 tablespoons liquid chlorine bleach to 1 quart (4 cups) water.

If mineral deposits have clogged your metal showerhead, mix ½ cup vinegar with 4 cups water in a large saucepan. Place showerhead in pan and make sure there is plenty of water to cover. Bring to boil and let simmer for 15 to 20 minutes. Rinse under cool water and dry completely. If your showerhead contains plastic parts and cannot be boiled, mix equal parts of vinegar and very hot (but not boiling) water. If the shower head has not cleared by the time the water cools, repeat.

The best time to clean the tiled walls of a bath or shower is right after you've finished using it, as the warm, steamy atmosphere will have loosened the dirt somewhat. If this isn't a convenient time for you, close the bathroom door and leave the shower on hot for several minutes before you start to clean.

For subtle air freshening that doesn't overwhelm, tuck an unused scented dryer sheet into the room—under the waste-basket, into the cabinet under the sink, in a frequently opened drawer, and behind the toilet tank are all good places.

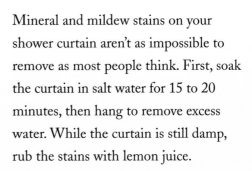

Soaking your shower curtain in salt water before hanging it up will help retard mildew.

Mineral and mildew stains on your shower curtain aren't as impossible to remove as most people think. First, soak the curtain in salt water for 15 to 20 minutes, then hang to remove excess water. While the curtain is still damp, rub the stains with lemon juice.

For continuous, low-cost air freshening, buy a small bottle of wintergreen oil at the drugstore, place a few drops on a cotton pad or ball, and tuck out of sight in a corner, drawer, or medicine cabinet.

I refuse to endanger the health of my children in a house with less than four bathrooms!

—Myrna Loy in *Mr. Blandings Builds His Dream House*, 1948

The Kitchen

Save shelf space by using utensils as décor. Bread and casserole baskets, copper molds, even pots and pans can all work to create an interesting wallscape. And if you have a prized collection of something—such as unusual cookie cutters or antique whisks—find a way to show it off.

If you've been making bread or pastry, your counter is likely coated with stuck-on bits of flour. For easy cleanup, soak a heavy terry-cloth towel under the hot water faucet and spread it over the mess. Let set until the towel has cooled, and you'll be able to wipe the counter clean without scraping.

To keep a ball of twine neat and handy, place the ball in an old teapot and thread the free end through the spout.

To keep your cutting board smelling fresh, cut a lemon in half and rub over the surface every now and then.

If you keep your dish drainer clean, you can use it for all sorts of jobs. It makes a great cooling rack for fresh-baked bread. And when you have a lot of fruit or vegetables to wash, set the drainer in the sink. This will keep your counters from getting wet and your just-cleaned fruit from touching the bottom of the sink. Best of all, the fruit will dry evenly and quickly.

An easy way to keep sponges and scrubbers fresh is to run them through the dishwasher every so often. If you're worried about them getting loose and clog-

ging the drain, use a bulldog clip or large safety pin to attach them to the rack.

Do you have a fire extinguisher in your kitchen? Why not? The time and money it takes to install one will never, ever compare with the repair costs of even a minor blaze, not to mention the personal safety aspects.

When you need to use a plunger on a clogged sink, rub some Vaseline around the rim—it will help keep the plunger from slipping.

To prevent your cutting board from sliding all over the counter, fold a piece of newspaper, wet it, and place it between the cutting board and the counter.

Sponges can be freshened by soaking in cold salt water.

A cheese grater coated with sticky cheese will be easy to clean if you grate some raw potato before you wash it.

To take grease out of the way fast, drain as much as possible off, then go over the pot or baking dish with a thick slice of lemon, or a used lemon turned inside out. Now wash as usual—you'll be surprised how much less grease you have to contend with.

The easiest way to unstick a jar lid is to run it under hot water, then try opening.

To keep plastic containers from discoloring when you store foods such as tomato sauce or curry in them, coat the inside with nonstick vegetable spray first.

What to do with all those plastic grocery bags you're saving for garbage liners? Fold them individually and store them in an empty tissue box or wipes container. You'll be surprised how many you can fit in, once the air is squeezed out.

If a wooden table has developed a white spot as a result of having something hot set on it, place a lump of butter in a piece of cloth and rub briskly for a few minutes. This will not always work, but it's worth trying.

If your kitchen chairs have vinyl upholstery, clean regularly to wash off body oils, which will make the vinyl hard and brittle. The proper way to clean: sprinkle vinegar or baking soda onto a damp cloth, go over chair thoroughly, then wash with a weak solution of water and dish soap and rinse.

Store plastic wrap in the fridge to keep it from sticking to itself when you unroll it.

A piece of plastic wrap that's hopelessly stuck to itself will be easy to smooth if you pop it into the freezer for 10 minutes or so.

A favorite old knife with a split wooden handle can be rescued by wrapping the handle tightly with duct tape. The tape is nearly waterproof and, if you don't leave the knife submerged, will last a long time before it needs to be replaced.

A heavy duty Ziploc-style freezer bag makes an excellent disposable pastry bag. Snip a small nick in a bottom corner and

PLASTIC WRAP

The first bit of the stuff that grew to be Saran Wrap was discovered in the 1930s by a college student whose job was cleaning beakers and test tubes for Dow Laboratories. One night he encountered a goo he couldn't wash off and dubbed it "eonite," after an indestructible material that, until then, existed only in the Little Orphan Annie comic strip. The Dow chemists named it Saran and developed it into a tough but oily, obnoxious-smelling film that was used by the military to protect aircraft wings from corrosive sea spray and by car manufacturers on interior upholstery. It burst onto the consumer market in 1956, when a clear, odorless version was approved for use with foods. The furor was only slightly smaller than Elvis, who had three hit songs that year—*Blue Suede Shoes*, *Hound Dog*, and *Love Me Tender*.

use as is, or snip a slightly larger corner to accommodate a pastry tip.

Place beaters in cool water as soon as you've finished using them, and they'll be easy to wash.

To save time and drawer space, consider keeping cooking utensils in wide-mouth jugs or crocks near the place they are used—ladles and turners by the stove, for example, and knives near the cutting board.

If your coffee maker is taking longer to brew coffee these days, it could be that mineral deposits are restricting the flow. To get rid of them, fill the water reservoir with white vinegar. Make sure the filter basket is in place but without a filter, and the carafe—with lid on—is on the warming plate. Turn on the machine, let half the vinegar go through, then turn off. Let set for 10 to 12 minutes, then turn back on and let the remaining vinegar flow through. If your machine has a lot of build-up, you may want to repeat the process. To rinse, process two reservoirs of tap water.

Don't throw away orange and lemon peels—feed them to your garbage disposal to keep it fresh-smelling.

To clean a garbage disposal, throw some ice cubes down it. The hardness of the cubes is just enough to scrape the blades without damaging them.

We've all been frustrated trying to open a Ziploc–style bag. To remedy the situation, snip a small notch into one of the edges, being careful not to cut into the zipper lines. The notch will serve as a tab, and help you open the bag easily.

Cereal-box liners can be handy things to save. Because they are tough and tear-resistant, they make excellent bags to use when you are crushing crackers or pounding meat. They're also good to use when you're flouring meat—just toss in the coating, seasonings, and meat, and shake.

Forget the fancy skimmers and grease "mops"—you probably already own the most efficient de-greasing gadget there is: a turkey baster. Just tilt the pan to let the grease form a well, squeeze the bulb of the baster, lower it into the grease and let it re-inflate. Tip the baster up as you withdraw it or hold a fold of paper towel over the end to keep the grease from leaking out.

A hinged tea infuser is a great way to sprinkle powdered or colored sugar evenly on cakes and cookies.

Top 10 Double-Duty Gadgets

BULLDOG CLIPS. Pin recipes to the stove hood while you're cooking, use them to pinch closed the pourspouts on milk and cream cartons to keep contents fresh

longer, or clip your long sleeves up while you're cleaning. Bulldog clips belong in every kitchen.

COLANDER. Can't locate the splatter screen? No problem—just invert your metal colander over the skillet. A large colander is also a handy container for stale bread when you are dying for bread-crumbs, and it's an excellent way to drain delicate hand-washed items that you don't want to wring or squeeze.

COTTON SWABS. Excellent for cleaning the crevices in waffle irons and other small appliances.

DENTURE TABLETS. Save scrubbing time—the same tablets that clean den-tures are great for loosening baked-on food from dishes and pans, getting rid of stains, and cleaning vases and glasses of mineral deposits left by water.

EGG SLICER. Think outside the shell on this one. Your egg slicer is a speedy way to slice cold boiled potatoes for home fries, as well as soft cheeses like mozzarella.

ICE CUBE TRAYS. Colorful, plastic, and dirt-cheap, ice cube trays are great for separating the screws, nuts, and bolts that come with assembly-required items. They make excellent drawer and workbench organizers, and are great for freezing homemade broth in small, ready-to-use servings. They're perfect paint palettes for little artists, and handy holders for beads, spare change, earrings, and other small items.

PAINTBRUSHES. Keep several inexpen-sive, stiff-bristled brushes—the kind you paint your walls with— on hand for all sorts of cleaning jobs. Use smaller ones to sweep your coffee grinder clean, and larger ones to brush dirt out of the corners and away from the baseboards before you scrub your floors.

PANTY HOSE. You know the dust is there, lurking in those tight spaces under beds, beneath and between appliances, as well as along the cupboards next to them. Wage war with old panty hose. Fit one leg inside the other and run a yardstick down the tube they form. Now you can get between those spaces and gather dust to your heart's content.

PAPER TOWEL

CORES. Use them as storage containers for saved plastic grocery bags, or for important keepsake documents such as diplomas, professional certificates, and children's art work. Wrap lengths of ribbon, twine, and holiday lights around them for tangle-free storage. Or slit the tube, insert a remnant of rolled fabric, tape closed, and write the yardage and fabric type on the outside for future reference.

TOOTHBRUSHES.

Don't throw away your old toothbrushes. Wash them thoroughly, then use them to clean hard-to-reach places like the bottoms of tall glasses, the grooves in appliances, and the bars of roasting racks. Used dry, they're excellent for dusting crumbs and debris from the seals around refrigerator and freezer doors.

SPACKLE KNIFE. A metal spackle knife is ideal for scraping unidentified gunk off surfaces such as cement walks, hardwood decks, and floors. Just cover the sharp corners with masking tape so you don't do any inadvertent damage.

Freshen your sink without damaging your pipes—before you go to bed, run cool water, then pour a handful of baking soda into the drain. Let set overnight, and flush with more cool water in the morning.

We all know better than to pour grease down a drain, but a fair amount makes its way there anyway. To forestall clogs, run some hot water down the drain when you're done cleaning up to move grease and food particles along.

Water spots on stainless-steel fixtures can be removed by polishing with a cloth moistened with rubbing alcohol.

Club soda is an excellent cleaner for stainless steel.

When you bake with the oven light on, be sure to lower the temperature setting for your oven. That little light casts a lot of heat and, depending on your oven, can make a 15- to 20-degree difference.

If you use an oven thermometer, don't place it at the front of the rack, since the space by the door is many degrees cooler than the oven's interior. Place the thermometer farther back and toward the center, where the food actually bakes.

Wiping oven walls with a cloth dampened with vinegar will help prevent grease build-up.

Baking soda works wonders on the

"What a husband you will be...in 1953!"

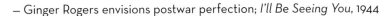

But I'm not talking about palaces and rainbows, Aunt Sarah. I'm talking about a home. A home like this with a kitchen and a stove and an icebox, and a husband, and a child.

— Ginger Rogers envisions postwar perfection; *I'll Be Seeing You,* 1944

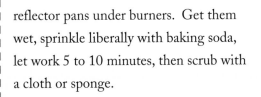

reflector pans under burners. Get them wet, sprinkle liberally with baking soda, let work 5 to 10 minutes, then scrub with a cloth or sponge.

To keep the oven clean while baking, place a cake pan $^2/_3$ full of water on the rack below whatever you're baking. Drips and spillovers will fall into the water, rather than scorching and smoking on the oven floor.

Oven racks with built-up burned or crusted food particles can be cleaned by placing the racks in a bathtub. Fill the tub with water to cover and add equal parts (about $^1/_4$ cup each) of vinegar and dishwasher detergent.

Sprinkle salt on spills and drips on the oven floor as soon as possible. Wipe up after the oven has completely cooled— a good share of the spill will come up with the salt. Finish by wiping with a damp sponge. If the spill wasn't too large, this may be all that's needed.

Few people know how to clean the oven window properly. First, only clean when the oven is completely cool, and never use glass cleaner alone, as this will lead to spotting. Instead, first spray the glass with oven cleaner and wipe clean. Then, and only then, apply glass cleaner for the final polish.

To clean a broiler pan, pour coffee grounds over it and rub well.

Use a small amount of baby oil on a paper towel to wipe fingerprints off stainless-steel appliances.

Corral small condiment jars that tip over or get lost in the back of the fridge, and put them in a small plastic bin that can be pulled out easily.

Line your vegetable drawer with two or three layers of paper towels—they help vegetables stay crisp by absorbing moisture and make cleanups easier.

A charcoal briquet or an open box of baking soda will absorb odors inside your refrigerator. When you're washing the interior walls and shelves, a bit of baking soda in warm soapy water will also help freshen the space.

Keep a running grocery list on your refrigerator door and make use of it. The time most needs come to light is when you're cooking, and if you wait to sit down and prepare a list all at once, you'll forget many of the items that occurred to you.

If possible, locate your refrigerator on a cool wall away from the stove, dishwasher, and other warmth-giving appliances. Your fridge won't have to work overtime.

Let foods cool down on the counter before putting them in the fridge—this conserves power and protects food already in the fridge from temperature fluctuations.

A freezer works more efficiently when it is full. A refrigerator works more efficiently when it is not full.

To clean and freshen a dishwasher, run a cup of

40 in. wide

COUNT THE IMPORTANT INCHES

18 in. oven

white vinegar through the entire cycle of the empty dishwasher.

Dried bay leaves in a kitchen drawer will discourage insects. Renew the leaves when they lose their pungent aroma.

To kill roaches, sprinkle boric acid on tops of cupboards, into crevices between cupboards, and wherever you see them scurry. It won't kill them on contact, as commercial spray will, but it will last far longer than a spray and, over the long run, be more effective. Since boric acid is toxic, make sure not to put it anyplace where children might reach it or where pets might get it on their paws and fur.

If you are having a bad roach problem, keep a spray bottle filled with ordinary soap and water handy. It's effective and non-toxic, though it may take a while to work.

To prevent ants from entering your home, paint your windowsills with lemon juice. Ants don't like the acidic juice and will not cross it. If ants have already invaded, a good way to round them up is to soak a sponge in sugar water and leave it on a plate on the counter. Within hours, the sponge will be laden with ants. Plunge it in boiling water, wash and wring out the sponge, and repeat the process until there are no more ants to attract.

Ants are allergic to cucumber skin. Place bits of it where they congregate and they will soon avoid the spot.

Table & Cookware

Buy an inexpensive file holder and store pot lids vertically. That way, you can pull out the one you need without disarranging the entire stack.

If your aluminum pans grow dull, you can restore them by boiling apple peelings in them.

Lengthen the life of new enamel saucepans by filling them with water and bringing to a slow boil. Let boil several minutes, remove from heat and let the water cool to room temperature before emptying. Your enamelware will be much more chip-resistant.

If you stack your pots and pans, line the insides of all but the top one with paper towels to prevent scratches and soiling.

If your teakettle shows traces of lime deposit, don't let the problem get out of hand. Use the kettle to boil potatoes in, or boil the peelings from carrots—

both methods will take away the lime. If potatoes and carrots aren't on the menu, fill the kettle with a solution of half water and half vinegar, bring to a boil, then remove from heat and let stand overnight.

Remove stains from copper and brass cookware with this easy homemade cleaner: add 1 tablespoon salt to ½ cup vinegar and mix in enough flour to make a smooth paste. Apply with a damp cloth and rub until stains vanish, rinse with cool water, and dry.

Harsh cleaners can darken aluminum. To keep it bright, go over it with a cloth dampened with lemon juice, rinse well, and dry.

If an aluminum pan has darkened, simmer some highly acidic food (such as tomatoes) in it. The darkening will decrease.

To keep cast-iron skillets from rusting, dry thoroughly, then rub the cooking surface with a paper towel moistened with salad oil.

Let metal cake pans and cookie sheets cool completely before washing—washing them while they are still warm will cause warping.

To remove baked-on food, rub casserole dishes with salt until the particles come free, then soak in a solution of warm water, baking soda, and dish soap before washing.

Glass baking dishes often acquire unattractive brown stains, but using scouring pads can leave scratches. Instead, scrub with dry baking soda each time you wash them. Eventually, the stains will be gone.

Sonny Rogers! I'll tell Mother you didn't dry the dishes!

—Shirley Temple rats out her brother; *What's To Do*, 1933

Hate scrubbing when food has crusted on glass baking dishes? Fill with warm water, add baking soda, and let soak before washing, or fill with warm water and add a denture tablet.

Rust on metalware can be taken care of by dipping the piece in cider vinegar. Set aside and let dry a few days, then wipe away the loosened particles.

Brass items that have developed corrosion spots can be aided by rubbing with a lemon rind dipped in salt. This should remove most of the spots.

To remove tarnish from brass, dip a piece of lemon rind in salt and use like an eraser.

Copper can be cleaned with a rubdown of salt and lemon juice.

Pewter is among the easiest of metals to clean. Just grab a cabbage leaf and rub, or rub with a handful of wood ashes dampened with cool water.

If you wash dishes by hand, don't waste time drying them—buy a large dish rack (two, if necessary) and let them air-dry. The only thing you really need to dry with a cloth is silver flatware, since it will tarnish if left to air-dry.

A water-stained glass or porcelain vase with a neck too small for a brush can be cleaned by pouring in a small amount of water and adding liquid toilet bowl cleaner to the level of the stains. Let stand 15 minutes, then empty and rinse with clean water.

A prized glass with a nick can be rescued with an emery board. Just smooth out the sharp edges as you would a jagged nail.

A scratch on a glass can be concealed by polishing with toothpaste.

Stacking glasses inside each other often leads to sticking, and glasses can crack if you force them apart. For easy uncoupling, fill the upper glass with cold water and dip the lower glass in very warm water. The lower glass will expand, the upper one will contract, and they'll slide apart easily.

Glassware, particularly vintage glassware, can crack if placed bottom first in very hot water. If hand-washing, let the glass adjust to the water by dipping it in sideways first.

To keep crystal sparkling, rinse in a solution of 3 parts warm water to 1 part vinegar. Let air-dry to avoid smudges.

When stacking dishes in a cupboard, place paper plates between delicate china plates to guard against scratches and nicks.

Tips for Silver

Get a head start on keeping your silver tarnish-free by rinsing thoroughly after washing, since even a small residue of soap will cause tarnishing.

If you use your good silver daily, rinse well, and wipe dry immediately, you will rarely have to polish it.

To remove tarnish from silverware, lay utensils in an aluminum pan. (It must be aluminum.) Sprinkle generously with baking soda, and place the pan in the sink. Pour boiling water over utensils, making sure they are completely covered. When the bubbling and fizzing stops, your silverware will be dazzling. Heavily tarnished silver may require a second treatment.

Egg stains can cause silver to tarnish quickly. To prevent this, sprinkle silverware with salt, then wash as usual.

To store silverware without tarnishing, wrap utensils individually in tissue paper and store in an airtight plastic container.

The same plastic wrap that keeps food fresh can keep your silver tarnish-free—just wrap tightly.

VOLLRATH WARE

s as easy to clean as your china
—and as beautiful!

YOU can't help exclaiming that Vollrath Ware is lovely! No woman can. But do you know that it is just as practical as it is beautiful? The smooth, glistening, non-porous surface of this famous old ware is as easy to clean as a china dish. Merely use soap and hot water. There's no scouring because food does not come in contact with anything but a sanitary vitreous surface. Properly handled, the smooth, hard surface of Vollrath Ware always stays smooth. It's easy on your hands, your time, and your temper!

This practical ware comes in a wide range of subtle, pastel-like colors that *harmonize* with all the approved modern decorative schemes. If your kitchen is already done in color, then it is just waiting for a set of Vollrath Ware in Color. Or if you would like to bring charm and cheer to a kitchen that's now drab, you will find this modern ware the magic touch. It will make you just as proud of your kitchen as you are of the rest of your home. And the gayety of color will have a daily influence on your happiness and good spirits.

At all good department stores—or your local house furnishing or hardware dealer's.

THE VOLLRATH CO.
ESTABLISHED 1874
SHEBOYGAN, WISCONSIN

The Vollrath Co., Sheboygan, Wis.

Please send me illustrated folders on Vollrath Ware and the modern kitchen.

Name_____

Street Address_____

City_____ State_____

Dealer's Name_____

Address_____

Food Tips A to Z

A

ASPARAGUS: To determine where the tasty part of the stem ends and the woody part begins, gently bend the spear until the stem snaps. This is the point at which you want to trim, and you can use the spear as a cutting guide for the rest of the bunch.

AVOCADO: Ripe avocados are soft to the touch. Unfortunately, so are bruised avocados. To tell the difference, try flicking the stem button at the narrow end of the fruit. If it is loose or falls off easily, the avocado is ripe. If the avocado is soft but the stem button doesn't wobble, it's probably bruised, and you should pass it by.

B

BACON: To separate frozen bacon without defrosting the whole package, hold a metal spatula over a stove burner or under scalding water, then gently slide between the slices.

Ricky Ricardo: What do you know about rice?
Fred Mertz: Well, I had it thrown at me on one
of the darkest days in my life.

—Desi Arnaz and William Frawley compare notes; *I Love Lucy*, 1951

BAKING POWDER: If you don't bake often, your baking powder may no longer be active. To test, place a few teaspoons in a cup of water. The fizzing should be instant and vigorous. If it isn't, buy a new can.

BAKING SODA: To see if baking soda is still active, place 2 teaspoons vinegar in a cup, add ¼ teaspoon baking soda, and stir. If the mixture doesn't fizz immediately, it's still a good odor absorber for the fridge, but buy a fresh box for baking.

BREAD: If you have a loaf of crusty, unsliced bread that's a bit stale, you can easily turn back the clock. Lightly dampen the loaf with a spray mister and place in a 350° oven for about 10 minutes. You'll have a loaf that tastes—and smells— deliciously fresh.

BREADING: Breading or flour-coating will adhere better if you refrigerate the meat, chicken, or fish for a few hours before cooking.

BROWN SUGAR: To keep brown sugar from going hard, store in a tightly sealed plastic container. Sugar that has gone hard can be softened in a microwave. But if you don't have a microwave, the old-fashioned way works just fine— grate the amount needed on a cheese grater.

BROWNIES: Faster, neater brownies are as close as your muffin tin. Fill cups about two-thirds full to make individual brownies that won't crumble or have to be cut. These brownies bake in about half the time, so you'll save oven work as well. When the brownies have cooled, store in a sealed plastic container.

BRUSSELS SPROUTS: You can increase the appeal of Brussels sprouts, cabbage, sauerkraut, and other vegetables that are associated with strong cooking odors by adding a few slices of red or green pepper to the cooking water. The peppers work to neutralize the odor.

BUTTER: To soften butter without melting it, place it in your oven with the oven light on for 15 to 20 minutes.

C

CAKE: Having a party? Cake layers can be made in advance, removed from the pan, individually wrapped in plastic wrap, and stored in the refrigerator 1 to 2 days before frosting.

CAKE FROSTING: To give iced cakes the smooth, glossy look of a professional bakery, apply frosting as usual, then run hot water over your metal spatula and go over the cake one last time to give it a finishing polish.

CAKE MIX: Boxed cakes can settle and form clumps that are difficult to mix. Before you add other ingredients, set your electric mixer on low and run to break up the lumps.

CELERY: If your celery has gone a bit limp, stalks can easily be re-crisped by immersing in an ice water bath for a few minutes before serving or slicing.

CHICKEN: Rubbing a wedge of lemon over chicken before you cook it will produce a juicier and more tender result.

CHOCOLATE: Instead of melting chocolate in a microwave or on the stove, turn on your electric coffee maker. Place chocolate in a heatproof glass or metal bowl, cover tightly with plastic wrap, and place the bowl on the heating plate. If you wish to keep the chocolate liquid for dipping, etc., remove the plastic wrap. Stir from time to time to make sure the chocolate isn't overheating.

COFFEE: To make coffee less acidic-tasting, sprinkle a pinch of salt in the basket along with the coffee and brew as usual.

COOKIES: Make cookie dough in large batches to save time in the future. Place cookie-sized lumps of dough on a baking sheet, freeze until solid, then transfer to a plastic container or heavy-duty Ziploc-style bag and store in freezer. Enjoy freshly baked cookies any time, without extra mixing. (See also Icebox Cookies.)

CORN ON THE COB: If you can't cook ears of corn right away, keep them crisp and sweet by trimming a small slice from each stalk end, then packing the ears upright, stalk ends down and husks still on, in a pan or jug filled with about 1 inch of water.

COTTAGE CHEESE: Strange but true: cottage cheese will stay fresh longer if you store the container upside down. It reduces exposure to air.

CREAM CHEESE: To soften cream cheese without making it too runny, place it in a Ziploc-style freezer bag, seal, and set in a bowl of hot water for a little while.

E

EGGPLANT: Wonder why some eggplants are seedy and bitter and others mild and almost seedless? The difference is the sex of the eggplants. Female eggplants are heavily seeded and turn bitter as they mature. Male eggplants, the ones you want to buy, have few seeds and don't become bitter. To tell the difference, examine the spot on the large, round end of the eggplant where the blossom once was. Female eggplants have a definite, dimple-like depression, while male eggplants have only a light mark or slight depression.

20 THINGS YOU SHOULD KNOW ABOUT EGGS

• Save money by knowing what's worth paying for. Brown eggs cost more but are no better than white eggs. They are not necessarily organic nor from free-range chickens. The breed of hen determines what color the shell is, and nothing more. Similarly, a deep yellow yolk is no more desirable than a pale yellow one. Savvy country folk have been taking advantage of us gullible city types for years on this one.

• Very rarely, you may get an egg with a small blood speck in it. This is meaningless. It has no bearing on the egg's taste or edibility, and need be removed only for aesthetic reasons. It may have occurred because the hen was startled during the egg's formation, or simply because the breed is prone to such speckling.

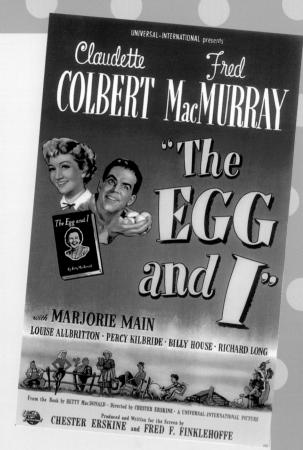

UNIVERSAL-INTERNATIONAL presents

Claudette COLBERT   Fred MacMURRAY

"The EGG and I"

with MARJORIE MAIN

LOUISE ALLBRITTON · PERCY KILBRIDE · BILLY HOUSE · RICHARD LONG

From the Book by BETTY MacDONALD · Directed by CHESTER ERSKINE · A UNIVERSAL-INTERNATIONAL PICTURE

Produced and Written for the Screen by
CHESTER ERSKINE and FRED F. FINKLEHOFFE

I really tried to like chickens. But I couldn't get close to the hen either physically or spiritually, and by the end of the second spring I hated everything about the chicken but the egg.

—Betty MacDonald; *The Egg and I*, 1945

- Eggs remain edible longer than most people think—more than 30 days after laying, if properly stored and handled. Although the appearance will not be quite as pleasing, taste and nutritional value will not suffer noticeably.

- To tell how fresh eggs are at the grocery store, touch them—the fresher the egg, the rougher the shell will feel. Eggs are also heavier when they are fresh and lighten as they age. Most eggs arrive at the grocery store within a few days of laying and are dated for freshness.

- To tell how fresh eggs are at home, place them in a bowl of room-temperature water. Very fresh eggs will lie along

the bottom. As the egg inside ages and shrinks, the air pocket at the broad end of the shell will expand, causing older eggs to float slightly. An egg several days old may bob at a 45-degree angle, while an egg weeks old will float perpendicularly, broad end up.

- Once out of the shell, a fresh egg has a tight, well-domed yolk and a gelatinous, even cloudy, white. In an older egg, the yolk will be flatter and will break more easily than the yolk of a fresh egg. The white will be clearer and thinner and will spread out more.

- Never store eggs in the refrigerator door. This is the warmest part of the appliance, usually about 45°F. Eggs should be stored at 38° to 40°F, which is the interior shelf temperature in most refrigerators.

- A basket of eggs may have rustic appeal, but it's best to store eggs covered, whether fresh or hard-boiled. The reason is that eggshells have microscopic air holes, and the air that seeps in can ruin their freshness and muddy their flavor with that of other foods.

- Eggs are best stored vertically, in

cupped cartons or trays. The narrow end should point down and the broad end up, so that the egg within is not sitting on the air pocket at the broad end.

• To separate an egg easily, crack open into a funnel. The white will slide through while the yolk remains in the funnel.

• Egg whites can be refrigerated in a covered container for up to one week. They can also be frozen and stored for up to one year.

• Eggs yolks will not last as long as whites in the refrigerator—just three days. Unbroken yolks should be covered with water in a covered container, while broken yolks should have a piece of plastic wrap pressed directly over their surface to prevent air from drying them.

• Unlike egg whites, egg yolks cannot be frozen as they are—they will turn thick and unusable. However, you can freeze them for cooking and baking needs. The trick is to add either salt or sugar to stabilize them—1 teaspoon salt or 1 tablespoon sugar per 6 beaten egg yolks. Just be sure to label the container as to the amount of egg and whether sugar or salt was added, so you'll know whether to use the yolks in sweet or savory dishes. (You can also freeze individual yolks in ice cube trays, then transfer frozen cubes to a plastic freezer bag.) Thaw frozen yolks in the fridge, 8 to 10 hours.

• Hate it when the yolks of hard-boiled eggs are way off center, making unattractive slices and lopsided deviled eggs? Shaking the egg gently before boiling will usually center the yolk.

• Perfect hard-boiled eggs are easy. Shells won't scorch or crack during cooking and you won't have to worry about the pan going dry if you adopt this simple method. Put eggs in a pan of cold water, with ample water to cover. Heat to boiling and as soon as a full, rolling boil is reached, remove the pan from the

HANDY YIELD CHART

	YOLK & WHITE (COMBINED)	YOLK	WHITE
Extra Large Egg	4 tablespoons	1⅓ tablespoons	2⅔ tablespoons
Large Egg	3¼ tablespoons	2¼ tablespoons	1 tablespoon
Medium Egg	3 tablespoons	2 tablespoons	1 tablespoon

burner and put the lid on. Let set for 15 minutes, then transfer to a bowl and cool under running water.

• Hard-boiled eggs will be easy to peel if you add salt to the water before you set the eggs to boil. This toughens the shell and makes it easier to remove in large pieces.

• A dropped egg can be a mess to clean up, so take the easy way out. Sprinkle the mess with a small handful of salt, wait ten minutes, and the egg will be much less soupy.

• Bigger isn't always better. If you use eggs primarily for cooking and baking, save money and cook better by buying medium or large eggs rather than extra large or jumbo. Since eggs today are generally larger than they once were, assume that eggs called for in vintage recipes are today's medium-sized, while contemporary recipes usually specify large eggs. Using larger or smaller eggs than directions call for could affect the results of certain recipes.

• Beat faster, higher-volume meringues by adding one teaspoon of cold water per egg white.

• When poaching eggs, adding a teaspoon of vinegar to the water will keep the white from spreading out.

F

FISH: When baking a large piece of fish that you want to serve intact, line the baking dish with cheesecloth. This will allow you to lift the cooked fish out and transfer it to a serving platter without it breaking apart.

FLOUR: Don't give bugs a chance. Transfer products such as flour, pancake mix, Bisquick, and the like to sealed canisters or heavy Ziploc bags. Boxed products can stay as they are until opened, but products that come in bags should be taken care of as soon as you bring them into the house.

FROZEN FOOD: Frozen fruit and vegetables will taste more like fresh if they are rinsed before defrosting. This will remove the ice particles that give food a stale, freezer-burned taste.

G

GRAVY: Instead of trying to get richly colored gravy by pan-browning your flour or roux, which can give a scorched taste, add a few drops of a browning agent, such as Kitchen Bouquet or Gravy Master.

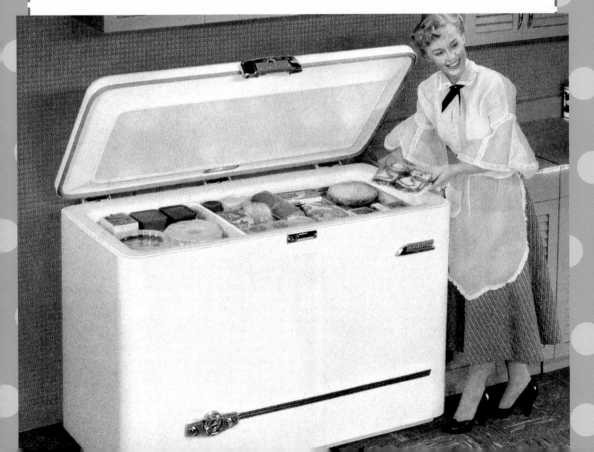

OUR GOVERNMENT
Says:

DON'T WASTE FOOD

BREAD CRUMBS

★ **SAVE DRY BREAD**
and Bread Crumbs

Make Delicious Leftover Bread Dishes!

JOIN the home-front army of housewives pledged against waste! Now that bread is enriched, more nutritious, you can't afford to waste any.

Leftover dry bread is delicious in bread pudding, crumb pie, as the crusty outside of fish, or as a "meat extender." Try "bread-baskets" filled with vegetables and served with nutritious "No Waste" SKINLESS frankfurters and wieners. (Recipe below.)*

Your government asks you to *buy carefully*; to ~~cook~~ *wisely* . . . maintaining the freshness and nutri~~tive~~ value of foods; to *cook correctly* . . . preser~~ving~~ vitamins and minerals; and to *save leftovers*. ~~This~~ Power will help win the war! Don't waste f~~ood.~~

Skinless - the No Waste food
TRADE MARK

● SKINLESS frankfurters are truly a nutritious "No Waste" food! They have no skin to peel (children love them) . . . 100% edible. You eat every bit you buy. No flavor is wasted, for SKINLESS don't split open. They waste no time, fuel, money, for they are quick to prepare and economical.

● Ask for your favorite brand of frankfurters and wieners made the "No Waste" SKINLESS way. They cost no more than ordinary frankfurters.

*Recipe: Remove crusts from 8 slices of day old bread. Press into greased muffin tin. Brush with melted butter. Bake 15 minutes in hot oven (425°F.)—until golden. Fill with creamed carrots, peas or other vegetables. Serve with SKINLESS frankfurters.

THE VISKING CORPORATION • 6733 WEST 65TH STREET, CHICAGO, ILLINOIS
Copr. 1943, The Visking Corporation. "VISKING" is the registered trade mark of The Visking Corporation

GREEN BEANS: Use scissors to trim and cut fresh green beans—much faster than a paring knife.

GUACAMOLE: Although the addition of lemon and lime juice to guacamole will help keep it from turning brown, browning will still occur if it has to be made ahead and held for several hours. For make-ahead guacamole that looks party-perfect, transfer it to the bowl you're going to serve it in (non-metal, please!), then cover it completely with a thin layer of sour cream. Make sure the sour cream goes right up to the sides of the bowl to form a seal—this will keep out air, which is what causes the browning. Garnish the sour cream with chives or slices of green onion, cover with plastic wrap, and store in the fridge until serving time.

H

HERBS: To chop fresh herbs quickly and easily, swap a pizza cutter for your knife. Roll the wheel firmly back and forth until the herbs are chopped to the fineness you desire.

HONEY: If your honey has begun to crystallize, make sure the cap is on tightly and hold the jar under hot running water. When all the crystals have dissolved, stir the honey well, and wash and dry the cap before replacing it. If you don't use honey often and crystals are always a problem, freeze small amounts and defrost as needed.

I

ICEBOX COOKIES: Homemade icebox cookies are supposed to be round but seldom turn out that way. For perfect treats, slit a cardboard tube (such as a paper towel core) vertically and line with plastic wrap. Evenly distribute dough to fill the tube. Bring edges of the tube back together, hold in place with rubber bands or tape, and refrigerate. When it's time to slice and bake, your cookies will be perfect rounds.

L

LEMONS: Have a hard time keeping lemons fresh and juicy until it's time to use them? Store uncut lemons in the refrigerator in a jar of water. They'll last longer and be much juicier than lemons stored in the vegetable drawer.

LEMON JUICE: Need just a few drops of lemon juice and don't want to waste the whole fruit? Pierce the whole, unpeeled

NEVER THROW AWAY A LEMON PEEL

Don't toss out your lemon peels. Here are some great uses for them:

• Float them in your bath for luxurious fragrance.

• Clean the inside of your teapot by adding 1 peel per 2 cups of warm water and soaking overnight.

• Feed them to your garbage disposal for a clean, fresh smell.

• Add to the water when you're washing greasy dishes or cookware—they're a natural grease fighter.

• Brighten your enamel sink by rubbing it with the inside of the peel. Sprinkle with cleanser, wait five minutes, then scrub. Your sink will be sparkling bright.

fruit with a toothpick or bamboo skewer, squeeze what you need, then use the toothpick as a plug to keep your fruit nice and fresh.

LETTUCE: If your lettuce is a bit wilted, submerge it in a bowl of cold water with some lemon juice and refrigerate for an hour. Drain, blot dry, and serve immediately.

M

MILK: To keep milk fresh longer, add a natural bacteria-fighter: salt. A pinch per gallon is all it takes.

MUFFINS: Muffins, cupcakes, and rolls sometimes stick to the tins. To get them out without pulling them apart, use a

curved, serrated grapefruit knife. Just slide the tip under the bottom, loosening gently, and you should be able to free them. You also can try setting the hot pan on a wet towel—the steam will loosen the muffins.

N

NUTS IN THE SHELL: Nuts are easier to shell if warmed in the oven for a few minutes immediately beforehand.

O

ONIONS: If your onions are a bit too strong, soaking cut pieces in cold water for 15 to 20 minutes will make them considerably milder.

P

PARSLEY: To keep parsley fresh longer, snip the stems and store upright in a glass of water, in the refrigerator. Change water frequently and discard wilted sprigs.

PASTA: Forget adding salt to water you cook spaghetti in. Add a spoonful of oil instead—it will prevent sticking and clumping and keep the pot from boiling over as well.

PEACHES: Fresh peaches will be easy to peel if you place them in a heat-proof bowl, pour boiling water in to cover, let stand one minute, then drain. The standing time is just long enough to loosen the peel without cooking the peaches. The same trick works for tomatoes.

KNOW YOUR POTATOES

• Keep potatoes from turning dark when you boil them by adding a small amount of milk or a teaspoon of vinegar to the water.

• Potatoes can be peeled ahead of time. Just cover the whole, peeled spuds completely with water, add a few drops of vinegar, cover, and store in the refrigerator until needed, up to three days.

• A large baked potato cut in half and wrapped in foil will bake twice as fast.

• A leftover baked potato can be reheated without drying it out if you dip it in water first.

• There are two secrets to great mashed potatoes. The first is not to waterlog the potatoes by overboiling them, and the second is to get rid of all the lumps before you start adding milk and butter.

• To keep potatoes hot while you whip them with a hand-held mixer, transfer the hot boiled potatoes to a metal bowl, but don't discard the water they've boiled in. Instead, lay a kitchen towel on the counter and set the pot on top of it. Now set the bowl of potatoes in the pot (make sure you use a bowl that has a large enough circumference and depth. The water in the pot will keep them piping hot.

• Adding a pinch of baking powder as you whip them will result in lighter, fluffier mashed potatoes.

PEPPERS: Extend the life of expensive vegetables like fresh red peppers. The minute you get home from the store, wrap the entire pepper tightly in plastic wrap—your pepper won't turn mushy and will stay fresh for days.

POPCORN: Store unpopped corn in the freezer. It will stay fresher and pop better.

R

RAISINS: If you're adding raisins to cookies or cake, plump them first by covering with water in a saucepan. Bring to a boil over high heat, remove from the burner at once, and let stand for about 10 minutes. Drain, blot with a paper towel, and add to your recipe. Instead of chewy little pellets, your raisins will be fat and moist.

RICE: For fluffier rice that won't clump, pre-rinse the rice before you cook it. Place rice in a bowl with cool water and swirl with your hand until the excess starch makes the water cloudy. Drain and repeat until the rinse water no longer clouds.

RISEN DOUGH: If your dough needs help rising, set it in the oven with a clean, damp towel over the pan and turn the oven light on.

S

SALAD: When you're too busy to make a tempting salad for dinner, buy bagged, washed, and chopped greens in the grocery aisle, then shop the salad bar for extras such as red and green pepper rings, sliced onions, mushrooms, cucumbers, and carrots.

SALT: Too much salt in the soup, stew, or sauce? And a teaspoon of sugar, or a teaspoon each of sugar and vinegar, and stir to dissolve. If your creation is too sweet, add a little salt or a teaspoon of vinegar.

SAUSAGE: To remove just one or two sausages from a package where the links have frozen together, run under hot water along the "seam" between links. Use a paper towel to dry the ones you want to stay frozen and return them to the freezer.

SPAGHETTI SAUCE: Upgrade your sauce by stirring in a spoonful of good balsamic vinegar—it will add a rich, complex note to your dish.

SHRIMP: Use a fine steel crochet hook for deveining—works like a charm.

SPICES: Revive whole spices that have

gone stale by toasting in a pan over low heat.

SWEET POTATOES: Uncooked yams and sweet potatoes will keep longer at room temperature than in a refrigerator.

T

TOMATO PASTE: Don't waste leftover tomato paste. Spoon 1- to 2-tablespoon portions into cupcake papers and freeze. When the paste is frozen solid, fold the sides of the papers to wrap. Place wrapped portions in a heavy-duty Ziploc style bag and freeze.

TOMATOES: Setting tomatoes on a sunny windowsill to ripen will only encourage soft spots. To ripen tomatoes without spoiling them, arrange them stem side up, not touching each other, out of direct sunlight.

Y

YEAST: If your yeast is old and doesn't seem to be working, add a pinch of ginger.

POPULAR MECHANICS

HOME KINKS

REG. U. S. PAT. OFF.

35¢
45¢ IN CANADA

1

2

3

4

How To Build

1 LAMP POST

From the Basement to the Great Outdoors

Even if you don't finish your basement, install a ceiling—it will insulate the floors above it, keep the unheated air where it belongs, and repay your investment many times over.

If your basement steps are poorly lit, paint the bottom step white or attach a reflector to let you know which step is the last.

If your basement steps are near your back door, hang a few coat hooks on the wall at the top of the steps. Jackets will be handy but out of sight.

The greatest waste of space is beneath the cellar steps. If you're not a do-it-yourselfer, it's worth every penny to have a handyman build shelves or custom-made pull-out bins to take advantage of every square inch.

Some Practical Uses of LUMINOUS PAINT

Keyholes and door-bell push buttons easily found in the dark if coated with luminous paint.

HOUSE LETTERS MADE VISIBLE AT NIGHT

Left, lowest tread of stairway, luminous at night, prevents stumbling. Right, lighting outdoor pump on dark night

For Rent INQUIRE RM 200

Signs and display cards in shop windows made noticeable

Switch plates in the house or garage seen readily visibly

Illuminating the hands and numerals of your clocks

"Spotting" fire extinguishers and fuse boxes

At summer camps, visitors will be better able to find boat landings if coated with luminous paint

7

Musty basement odor can be diminished by filling a wide-mouth jar, such as a mayonnaise jar, with vinegar, leaving the lid off, and setting it in an out-of-the-way corner.

Brass doorknobs and door knockers can be cleaned and polished by rubbing with salt and vinegar.

Go over window and door screens with a damp sponge to re-move dust and pollen.

If the key to your front door sticks and the mechanism is stiff, dip the key in oil. This is an excellent way to lubricate the lock and may be all that's needed.

If your awnings, patio umbrella, or lawn furniture get left out in the rain, let them dry completely before folding away. This will prevent rot and mildew and preserve their life.

If you have a heated garage, don't waste money overheating it in the winter. Keep it no warmer than your refrigerator and you'll be fine.

Have trouble finding the garage light, a doorknob, or a keyhole in the dark? Try a dab of luminous paint.

If you have to put two cars in a garage that's a tight squeeze, try this. When both cars are parked correctly, attach a pingpong ball or similar object to a long length of string. Hang the string from the rafters at a place where it lines up with a specific part of the car— such as the center of the hood or front left headlight—so you'll know exactly where to park when you pull in. Do this for both cars.

Small oil spots on a garage floor can be removed by sprinkling with kitty litter to absorb, then sweeping up. If this doesn't work, try laying a thick section of your daily newspaper atop the spill and adding just enough water to saturate the paper. Stand on the paper for a few minutes to make sure it is pressed firmly against the oil spot. Allow to dry completely, and remove—the paper should have blotted up the oil.

Larger oil spots on the garage floor require a multi-step process. First, set up your work area: remove all vehicles from the garage, open the doors for ventilation, and put on a pair of rubber gloves. Now, pour some mineral spirits on the stain, allow to soak for 30 minutes, then scrub the spot with a stiff bristled brush, using more mineral spirits. Use newspapers to blot up the mineral spirits and as much of the stain as possible. While the area is drying completely, mix one gallon of cold water with laundry detergent. Use this solution to thoroughly wash the treated area. If some of the stains remain, wash a second time.

A little care with your garage floor will help your entire house stay cleaner. Treat the floor with a cement sealer, and when it has dried thoroughly, finish with a light coating of wax. Both steps will help repel grime and dust, and a cleaner garage floor reduces the amount of dirt that will eventually be tracked inside.

Ants dislike chalk. Use a stick of plain white chalk to draw a perimeter around the patio, deck foundations, or picnic table.

This is Levittown! All yours for $58. You're a lucky fellow, Mr. Veteran. Uncle Sam and the world's largest builder have made it possible for you to live in a charming house in a delightful community without having to pay for them with your eye teeth.

—The first ad for paradise; *The New York Times*, March, 1949

Washing bamboo and rattan patio furniture with salt water will not only clean it but also retard discoloration.

Wicker, rattan, and bamboo lawn furniture should be rubbed with lemon oil from time to time to counteract the sun's drying.

If you live in a cold climate, move wicker, rattan, and bamboo lawn furniture into the garage or basement for the winter, or store in a protected shed. The furniture should not be allowed to freeze, as this promotes cracking and splitting and shortens the life of your pieces.

To remove rust spots from metal furniture, try using a stiff brush and mineral spirits.

Save water and yard work by letting your grass grow a bit longer. Longer grass needs less frequent watering.

To keep weeds from growing in the cracks of a cement driveway, generously sprinkle the

cracks with salt or baking soda from time to time.

To kill weeds growing between the cracks in driveway and walks, pour boiling salt water over them.

Dry lawn tools thoroughly to keep them rust-free. If a bit of rust does develop, cover with a bit of machine oil and scrub with a stiff-bristled brush.

To keep garden tools shipshape over the winter, rub the blades with a generous coating of machine oil before putting them into storage.

A splintered wooden handle on a lawn tool can be repaired by sanding out the splinter, then rubbing the handle with linseed oil to seal the wood. To prevent future splinters, sand and oil the handles of all your wooden garden tools once a year.

If mice are nesting in your plants or hedges, scoop some used cat litter, saturated with urine, into a plastic bag and leave the open bag by the plants for a few days. The rodents are sensitive to cat scent and will relocate to an area they deem safer.

And now the *cellar* becomes another *room*

here's a game of billiards in full
g—dad and the boys are having
time of their lives. The cellar has
me a "den"—and exclusive terri-
for the men of the family.

ow much the new "Thatcher"
e Boiler has contributed to this
sformation you can readily see for
rself. And the house—the great
house above—from mother's sew-
room to the children's nursery—
nug and warm like a woolly blan-
no matter how much the chill
ds blow outside.

And throughout the house
you will find the new Thatcher
"Gothic" Radiators—gracefully
proportioned, decorative, and most
efficient in heat delivery. The house
that "Thatcher" heats is always warm
—never cold, for the powerful
Thatcher boiler with its famous

"staggered fire travel" drives
the heat upward with unfailing
persistency.

Write us today for illustrated booklets on both
the new Thatcher "Elite" red enamel jacketed
Boiler and the new Thatcher "Gothic" Radiator.

THE THATCHER COMPANY
39-41 St. Francis St., Newark, N. J.
New York—21 West 44th St.
Chicago—341 No. Clark Street

THATCHER
Elite ENAMEL JACKETED Boilers

"I'm sure I get *The most for my money!*"

says Mrs. Jeanne Endres, of Birmingham, Michigan
As told to Constance Lewis,
Women's Page Editor, Birmingham Eccentric

"I look at wartime food shopping this way: I want to be ab
to select from a real variety of good, nourishing foods
keep my family healthy. And I also want to know that I'
getting the utmost for my money to keep my food budg
in bounds ... for good value is so important these days. :
I do *all* my food shopping at my A&P Super Market. Th
selection of good things to eat — from appetizers throu
main-course dishes to desserts—that I find at my A&P Sup
Market, reduces my problems to merely a matter of choice
I can choose confidently because I know I'm making im
portant savings on practically every purchase I make"

SUBURBAN DETROIT PRESENTS Jeanne Endres, A&P enthusiast whose hobbies include gardening and cooking ... one-year-old Anthony (Andy) whose chubby good looks verify his mother's knowledge of vitamins, minerals and well-balanced meals ... and her husband Anthony (Tony) whose spare hours are devoted to photography. Mr. Endres (below) is a designer employed by a leading maker of oil filters for automatic pilots in Uncle Sam's bombers. Jeanne and Tony, both University of Michigan graduates, find A&P shopping worthwhile because they insist on good food and income-protecting low prices.

Giving homemakers the most possible in good, nutritious food for each dollar they spend has been the biggest single factor in the success of A&P. And today in wartime, as in peacetime, A&P is determined to make your food money buy the utmost.

Save up to *25%** ON MANY FINE FOODS

*Many A&P brands (sold only at A&P) bring you sav-ings up to 25% compared to prices usually asked for other nationally known products of comparable quality. These savings are yours because A&P brings these good things direct from their source to you with many un-necessary in-between expenses cut from their cost.

33 Ann Page Foods	Nectar and
Eight O'Clock, Red Circle	Our Own Teas
and Bokar Coffees	Marvel "Enriched" Bread
Jane Parker Cakes, Rolls	White Sail Household
and "Dated" Donuts	Products
7 Sunnyfield Cereals	Sunnyfield Flours
A&P Canned Fruits and	and many other
Vegetables	fine foods

A&P SUPER MARKETS

A&P ESTABLISHED 1859

Money Savers

If you're thinking of a major change in your residence—whether it's buying a new home, selling your current home, or a renovation—take advantage of the buy, sell, and remodel shows on cable TV channels such as HGTV, Discovery Home, and The Learning Channel. Even if you have to up your service tier to get them, these shows will actually teach you something, and the few hundred dollars you spend will pay off in thousands saved.

The easiest way to put the brakes on spending is to figure the cost in dollars you have to earn to buy a particular item. Start by knowing what percent of every dollar you earn goes to taxes (including Social Security). Add this to the price of the item, along with any sales tax you'll pay. You may find that buying a $10 item may mean you'll have to earn $15 to be left with the $10 needed to make the purchase.

We often buy ourselves little things to compensate for not buying the big thing we feel we can't afford. However, try keeping track of what you spend on all those little treats for a few weeks or a month—you may find that foregoing the things that don't really matter will move you much closer to being able to buy the big thing that does.

If you're on a tight budget and have to bring something to a dinner party, ask to bring dessert. Everybody loves dessert, and it's almost invariably the least expensive course on the menu. We've shown up at elegant parties with a cheesecake that cost less than $4 to make and gotten more accolades than the friend who arrived with a $20 bottle of wine.

Keeping the thermostat at 70°F rather than 75°F in the winter can lower heating bills by up to 15 percent.

To lower winter fuel costs, draw shades and lower blinds as soon as the sun sets to keep cold air out. For climate control in the summer, reverse the process—deploy shades and blinds during the brightest, hottest part of the day to keep your rooms cooler.

For maximum efficiency and fresher air, clean or replace filters in your furnace and air conditioning units frequently—once a month for the furnace in cold-weather months, and the same for air conditioners in the summer.

Don't be a dim bulb when it comes to lighting—one high-wattage bulb will produce half again as much light as several bulbs of the same combined wattage.

Dust the lightbulb as well as the lamp. Even a fine coating of dust will significantly reduce light output.

Lose the habit of letting water run to get a cool drink—you're sending money down the drain. Instead, keep a bottle of water in the refrigerator.

Most people know that storing batteries in the freezer will lengthen their life. But did you know that laying them in a sunny windowsill for a day will boost their energy?

Shopping online can be a tremendous money saver, especially at Web sites that offer heavy discounts, free shipping, or coupon incentives. Be sure to sign up for e-mail notifications for special sales and rebate offers—some Web sites have sales so frequently there's no point in ever paying full price again.

Shopping online can also be unexpectedly expensive. Before you hit the "Place My Order" button, make sure you know the cost of shipping and handling charges. Some online companies offer discount prices, only to make it up by overcharging for processing.

Never have a credit card that's just a credit card. Shop for ones that give the best perks and rewards. Changing cards won't hurt your credit.

Take a calculator to the grocery store and don't be afraid to do the math. "Economy"-sized products aren't always cheaper than smaller sizes.

Plan main dishes around what's on sale, or what you bought on sale and put in your freezer. Typically, when beef, pork, or chicken go on sale, the savings are far more than a few cents—savings of 30 to

Ricky Ricardo: Fred, how often is Ethel's checking account overdrawn?

Fred Mertz: Never.

Ricky Ricardo: Never? How do you manage that?

Ethel Mertz: It's easy. I never had enough money at one time to open a checking account.

—Desi Arnaz, William Frawley, and Vivian Vance find the key to fiscal responsibility;
I Love Lucy, 1953

50 percent are more the norm, and since protein is the most expensive part of the meal, it's your best chance to save big.

Books, magazines, newspapers, CDs, DVDs—these are just some of the things most people pay for that your library has on loan for free.

One of the most effective ways to save money is to learn to cook. Convenience foods are tremendously expensive, and usually have unhealthy additives (like salt and sugar) you wouldn't put in yourself. You don't need

to become a Cordon Bleu chef to save, either. Even a few simple tricks, such as making your own salsa instead of buying it or substituting homemade for microwaved popcorn, will save you hard-earned dollars.

A tight budget is no reason to forego the pleasure of eating out. Just make it lunch instead of dinner. Even on the weekends, lunch is a far better buy.

Rotate the toys. Children are always wanting something new, and it's hard to tell them no. The truth is, most kids have more toys than they know what to do with. Pack up some of them (not their everyday favorites) and put them away for a while. When you hear the "I'm bored" chant set in, bring out something they haven't seen recently, and put something else away in its place. For a week or two, the forgotten toy or game will be in favor again.

Another way to save money on children's toys is to help them be creative with toys they already have. Barbie doesn't always need a new outfit or yet another Barbie to compete with. Sometimes she needs a little girl with some fabric and a needle and thread, just as action figures and miniature race cars need little boys to build skyscrapers and garages out of cardboard and crayons.

Most of us go through shampoo and conditioner twice as fast as we need to because it's human nature to squirt out a generous dollop. To save money, mix

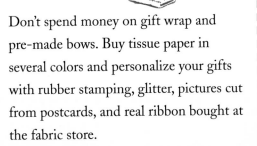

products in a 1:1 ratio with water and use that instead.

Unless there's something specific on your "to buy" list, discard all catalogs you receive in the mail, as well as e-mail notices.

Don't spend money on gift wrap and pre-made bows. Buy tissue paper in several colors and personalize your gifts with rubber stamping, glitter, pictures cut from postcards, and real ribbon bought at the fabric store.

If you have more time than money to spend, give handmade gifts. Food gifts—such as fudge and butterscotch sauces for an ice cream lover, as well as handiwork from crafts and hobbies, are easy to personalize, and most people would rather have them than something bought in a store.

Bargains are hard to resist, but be realistic about how much of a given product you are likely to use in the future. If it won't get used in a reasonable period of time, pass it by. There will be other sales.

HOME KINKS

REG. U. S. PAT. OFF.

Miscellaneous

To tighten a drawer or cupboard knob when the screw is loose, remove the screw from the knob, dip in glue, then reassemble and allow to dry before using. The glue should tighten the screw's grip.

When you need to drive a nail into a wall, mark the spot with a small "X" of tape. Not only will it guide the placement of the nail, but it will also keep the paint, wallboard, or plaster from cracking and flaking.

To avoid splitting a narrow piece of wood when you nail it, push the nail into a cake of soap first. This will make the nail smoother and less likely to split the wood.

To loosen a screw that's tightened, try sprinkling a few drops of hydrogen peroxide on the screw. Let sit a few minutes and try again. If the screw still won't budge, heating the edge of your screwdriver should help.

If a tube-style fluorescent light darkens at one end, try reversing the tube.

I can't figure her out. She's got a home to clean, meals to cook, dishes to wash, you two kids to look after, floors to scrub— what more does she want?

—William Bendix lives *The Life of Riley*

To anchor tapers so they won't tip, melt a few drops of wax into the empty holder, then insert the candle. The hardened wax will hold it firmly.

If your candles have become soiled, moisten a folded paper towel or cotton ball with isopropyl alcohol and gently wipe the dirt away.

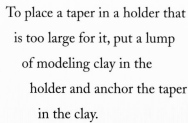

To place a taper in a holder that is too large for it, put a lump of modeling clay in the holder and anchor the taper in the clay.

To remove stubs that have melted into the candleholder, hold the candleholder under hot water for a few minutes, then *gently* insert the tip of a steak knife or paring knife to loosen.

Cut flowers add beauty to any room. To make the most of your blooms, add a charcoal briquet to the water—it will keep the water fresh-smelling and make the flowers last longer.

Okay, this isn't a household hint, but we thought it was too good not to pass along. For ballpoint-pen ink marks on your hands, moisten the mark with water and erase with the head of a sulphur-tipped match. Works like a charm!

Index